Journey of Faith

FOR CHILDREN

INQUIRY LEADER GUIDE

Liguori
PUBLICATIONS
A Redemptorist Ministry

Journey of Faith for Children, Inquiry Leader Guide (826368)

Imprimi Potest: Stephen T. Rehrauer, CSsR, Provincial, Denver Province, the Redemptorists

Imprimatur: "In accordance with CIC 827, permission to publish has been granted on April 18, 2017, by Bishop-Elect Mark S. Rivituso, Vicar General, Archdiocese of St. Louis. Permission to publish is an indication that nothing contrary to Church teaching is contained in this work. It does not imply any endorsement of the opinions expressed in the publication, nor is any liability assumed by this permission."

Journey of Faith © 1993, 2005, 2017 Liguori Publications, Liguori, MO 63057.
To order, visit Liguori.org or call 800-325-9521.

Text: Adapted from *Journey of Faith for Adults* © 2000 Liguori Publications.

Editor of the 2017 *Journey of Faith for Children*: Theresa Nienaber-Panuski.
Design and production: Wendy Barnes, Lorena Mitre Jimenez, John Krus, and Bill Townsend.
Cover image: Soloviova Liudmyla/Shutterstock. Interior illustration: Jeff Albrecht

Printed in the United States of America
21 20 19 18 17 / 5 4 3 2 1
Third Edition

Contents

Welcome to *Journey of Faith!*

Liguori Publications is dedicated to providing parishes with quality resources like *Journey of Faith*. Since 1993, *Journey of Faith* has established itself as a trusted and beloved program for catechists to guide participants through the RCIA process. As the Catholic Church takes on the challenges and graces of each generation, *Journey of Faith* has been carefully developed to help you meet the changing needs of adults, teens, and children who are inquiring about and seeking initiation into the Catholic Church—ever ancient, ever new.

The *Journey of Faith* program is cohesive, comprehensive, and flexible. The forty-eight catechetical lessons and three corresponding *Leader Guides* create a practical and attractive formation process for today's team leaders, catechists, and participants. All the materials are referenced to the *Catechism of the Catholic Church* and have been granted an *imprimatur* from the Archdiocese of St. Louis.

Unbaptized children over the age of seven are to be considered catechumens. Liguori offers *Journey of Faith for Children* to any child needing formation or sacraments. All *Journey of Faith for Children* products are available in Spanish under the title *Jornada de Fe para niños*.

We hope you enjoy using *Journey of Faith* and find it enlightening and engaging for all. To see our entire collection of sacramental preparation titles, parish subscriptions, formation and spirituality books, and more, please visit Liguori.org to contact us for a copy of the latest catalog.

—The editors

An Overview of the RCIA

The Historical Development

The decision to become a member of the early Christian community bore serious ramifications. Becoming Christian meant a break with one's background and often required fracturing relationships with the non-Christian members of one's family. In many cases, this decision meant a willingness to suffer persecution or even death, as seen in the example of the martyrs Perpetua and Felicity. Perpetua, a noblewoman of Carthage and mother of an infant son, and Felicity, a pregnant slave woman, both refused to denounce Christianity and were subsequently martyred during the public games in the amphitheater around the year 200.

Just as the decision to become a Christian was not made lightly, the formation process wasn't quick or easy. Catechumens—those in the process of preparing for baptism—were invited into a step-by-step journey of three or more years with the community before achieving full membership. During this process they were expected not only to begin to accept Christian beliefs but also to begin to live the Christian life. The community shared their faith with the catechumens and celebrated each step along with them.

One period of this preparation has remained throughout the centuries: the season of Lent. Originally this time was one of immediate preparation for baptism, which was celebrated at the Easter Vigil. During Lent, the entire Christian community, especially the catechumens, devoted themselves to prayer, fasting, and self-scrutiny. For those already baptized, it was a time to remember and renew their original commitment.

During the solemn Easter Vigil, the catechumens—now called the elect—received the sacraments of initiation (baptism, confirmation, and Eucharist) and were welcomed into the community. As a rule, this initiation was celebrated at the Easter Vigil only. Formation of the newly baptized did not end with the rites of Holy Saturday night, however, but continued with further instruction and the daily living out of Christian values.

This process began to change in the fourth century, when periodic persecution of Christians was replaced by tolerance. Because of the favor many emperors showed toward it, Christianity became fashionable, and many people began entering the catechumenate for social and political reasons. As a result, the pattern and standards for formation gradually transitioned to the point where, by the fifth century, the rites of initiation were separated into the three sacraments we know and celebrate today. Infant baptism became the norm, and the catechumenate vanished.

The Church published the first *Roman Catechism* in 1566, following the Council of Trent. This book of teachings was presented in question-and-answer form and was used for instruction of the faithful. Such catechisms later became the foundation for what came to be called "convert classes." Using a teacher-student model, the priest would meet with interested parties and assist them in memorizing certain prayers and learning the material in the catechism. The duration of the process, the material to be covered, and the format were left to the priest or parish custom, with few outside directives given.

Successful completion of these classes meant either baptism or formal reception into the Catholic Church. This event was usually celebrated in a private ceremony, with only close family in attendance. Those received into the Church would be confirmed by the bishop at the cathedral or would receive the sacrament in their local parish whenever the bishop came to confirm the schoolchildren. Follow-up for the new Catholics, if any, might consist of being sent to a formal course in liturgy, Scripture, dogma, or morality.

Following World War II, a call for a change in the formation of new Catholics came from the Church in Africa. They began to use the ancient form of the catechumenate to provide stability in formation and a period of time for faith to mature. The Second Vatican Council called for a thorough revision of all the rites (Constitution on the Sacred Liturgy [*Sacrosanctum Concilium*], 4), and a committee that engaged in a formal study and revision of the methods leading to baptism or reception into the Catholic Church was formed. This study resulted in the promulgation of the *Rite of Christian Initiation of Adults (RCIA)* in 1972.

Thus the catechumenate was restored: a process of formation, sanctified by various liturgical rites that mark progress in the journey of faith and culminate in full membership in the Catholic Christian community. An integral part of the revision is that the whole process and its rites are to be celebrated with and in the context of the local parish community and diocese.

The Scholastic or Ongoing Catechumenal Model

The catechumenate is considered a *process*, not a *program*, because it is a spiritual journey that varies according to time, place, and individual needs. It primarily focuses on:

- *Faith development* (rather than mastery of doctrine) and maturing in one's relationship with God.

- *Building and nourishing relationships*, not only among the participants and leaders but within the parish community and the universal Church.

Most U.S. parishes follow an academic schedule that begins in September and runs through May. However, this approach can make the process feel forced, rushed, or like a course of study that focuses on the *content* of the faith rather than the participant's experience of a *deepening conversion* and growing commitment. For this and other reasons (for example, risking that the *Catechism* becomes the main "course text" rather than the *Lectionary*), many pastoral ministers prefer an ongoing model for the process. *Journey of Faith* can be applied well to a number of models and provides a built-in flexibility that supports many formats.

Flexibility is one of the greatest assets of the RCIA. Within certain parameters, the pastor is given the freedom to accommodate the rites according to his judgment in order to fit the needs of the participants and parish. You, as catechists and team leaders, are encouraged to use your judgment in developing a process suited to the needs of both catechumens and candidates.

The Periods

This section provides detailed information on the periods of the RCIA. A basic orientation to the RCIA process is included in lessons Q1, "Welcome to the RCIA," and C1, "The RCIA Process and Rites." Together these lessons build a foundation for the participants as they begin their faith formation. The corresponding lesson plans support you, the leader, and offer program-specific notes.

Evangelization and Precatechumenate (Inquiry)

The first period is called *inquiry* or the *precatechumenate*. During this period, inquirers form relationships with one another and with their catechists. The sessions are informal and often center upon questions such as:

- What is faith?

- Who is God, and why does God care about me?

- How does the Church understand the Bible and the sacraments?

- What are the roles of Mary and the pope?

- Why are there statues in Catholic churches?

Each inquirer will examine the Church and the ways in which its members worship together and live the Christian faith. First impressions of the parish and of all involved are very important. The period culminates in the inquirer's decision to enter the catechumenate, the period of formal preparation for entrance into full membership in the Catholic Church.

Catechumenate

The *rite of acceptance* marks the beginning of the catechumenate, a period of study and reflection on the faith. At this point, the inquirers become catechumens. Candidates (those already baptized but preparing for full membership in the Catholic Church) formally enter the RCIA process through the *rite of welcoming*. Both publicly state their intention to continue their formation, and the community supports them in their journey. Sponsors will act as companions and models of faith and lend their personal support.

The length of this period is determined by the needs of each participant and of the community. It can last anywhere from several months to a couple of years. During this time, the catechumens and candidates:

- learn Catholic beliefs.

- are exposed to various forms of prayer.

- join the community in worship, social events, and charitable activities.

- participate in the apostolic life of the Church.

During the catechumenate, catechesis usually takes place during the Sunday liturgy. The participants are prayerfully dismissed after the Universal Prayer (Prayers of the Faithful); the catechists, and sometimes the sponsors, join them in reflecting upon the day's readings and connecting them to their faith and the life of the Church.

> "There should be celebrations of the word of God that accord with the liturgical season and that contribute to the instruction of the catechumens and the needs of the community….Celebrations of the word may also be held in connection with catechetical or instructional meetings of the catechumens, so that these will occur in a context of prayer."
>
> *RCIA chapter of The Rites, Volume One (RCIA), 81, 84*

Purification and Enlightenment

When the catechumens and candidates are ready to make a formal request for the sacraments of initiation, and when the catechists and godparents are ready to recommend them to the bishop and to the parish community for full membership, the *rite of election* is celebrated. This celebration is generally held on the first Sunday of Lent. The *rite of election* marks the beginning of the *period of purification and enlightenment*, the time of immediate preparation for initiation or full reception at the Easter Vigil. *Journey of Faith* refers to this period as enlightenment.

The beginning of Lent signals a forty-day "retreat" in which the parish joins the elect in preparing for the mysteries celebrated at the Easter Vigil. The RCIA sessions are marked by an increased emphasis on prayer and the interior life rather than on an accumulation of knowledge. Many parishes allow time for a day of prayer designed for the elect and their supporters. On the third, fourth, and fifth Sundays of Lent, the scrutinies are celebrated during the liturgy. These rites are prayers of healing in which the elect, as well as the faithful, are reminded that everyone needs continued healing, conversion, and reconciliation.

Postbaptismal Catechesis (Mystagogy)

- The Easter Vigil does not mark the end of the RCIA process but the beginning of a commitment to a lifelong discovery and living out of the Catholic Christian tradition. The fifty days from Easter to Pentecost are called the period of *mystagogy*, a Greek word meaning "entering into the mysteries." In the early Church, this time was used to explain the mysteries of the sacraments. Today this period serves as a time for today's neophytes (newly converted) to:

- continue to gather, pray, and nourish their faith.

- deepen their experiential understanding of God's word and the sacraments.

- center more on the apostolic or social justice aspects of Catholic Christianity.

- claim a new role of service in the community. (All Catholics are invited to active participation in parish life, which includes worship, stewardship, and fellowship.)

Sponsors and Godparents in the RCIA

> "A person to be baptized is to be given a sponsor who assists an adult in Christian initiation….A sponsor also helps the baptized person to lead a Christian life…."
>
> *Code of Canon Law, 872*

Prior to the rite of acceptance, RCIA sponsors should be chosen for all catechumens. Sponsors represent the parish community and assist the larger Church in preparing the catechumen for baptism (here, initiation), testify to his or her faith, and promise to assist him or her in living the Catholic faith.

Canon 874 lists the basic criteria for sponsors. These guidelines are the same for baptismal godparents and confirmation sponsors, though the roles are somewhat different:

1. The sponsor should be designated or invited by the catechumen or candidate. If he or she doesn't have someone in mind, the RCIA leader(s) or pastor will select an appropriate person from a voluntary pool of parishioners. This is similar to parents choosing godparents at the time of their child's baptism.

2. The sponsor must be at least sixteen years old—in other words, mature enough to understand and fulfill this important role.

3. The sponsor must be a confirmed Catholic "who leads a life of faith"—someone who has already committed to and experienced the Catholic faith journey.

4. No sponsor can be subject to a Church penalty such as excommunication.

5. The sponsor cannot be the participant's parent. In the case of infant baptism, the

parents already have a unique and important role to play. Some adult catechumens desire to have their spouse or a close friend or relative as a sponsor. This is generally discouraged, but RCIA leaders and pastors can help the catechumen decide whether the potential sponsor is sufficiently experienced and objective to fulfill this role.

RCIA leaders should develop a list of parishioners who are willing to become sponsors and maintain those connections as new inquirers arrive each year. It is important for sponsors with no prior relationship to the catechumen to realize that they are committing to an *ongoing* spiritual relationship. While their ecclesial role technically ends at the rite of election, sponsors often serve as, or stand in for, godparents, whose support lasts a lifetime.

Godparents are chosen before the rite of election (*RCIA* 123). Like sponsors, they will encourage, inspire, and even hold the elect accountable to remain faithful to Christ. Whenever possible, encourage the catechumens to use their RCIA sponsor as a baptismal godparent. Additional guidance for godparents can be found in the *Journey of Faith for Children, Catechumenate Leader Guide*.

The Rites

Rite of Acceptance
Into the Order of Catechumens

This rite marks the first transition in one's journey—the move from being an interested inquirer to an active catechumen. (For candidates seeking full communion in the Church, the *rite of welcoming* is used. The combined rite is detailed in *RCIA* 507 and following.) The importance of this step is rightly recognized by the Church.

1. Symbolizing movement into the community, those asking to be received, along with their sponsors, begin by standing at the doors of the church (*RCIA* 48). The celebrant introduces them to the worshiping community, and asks, "What do you ask of the Church?" They state their desire for initiation, implying their intent to live, learn, and love with the community.

2. The Sign of the Cross is marked on each forehead, symbolizing the love and strength of Christ that accompanies each person (*RCIA* 54–55). This sign of faith may also be marked on their:

   a. ears (to hear the Lord's voice),

   b. eyes (to see God's glory),

   c. lips (to respond to God's word),

   d. heart (that Christ may dwell there),

   e. shoulders (to bear the gentle yoke of Christ),

   f. hands (that their work witnesses to Christ), and

   g. feet (to walk in Christ's way) (*RCIA* 56).

3. After the signing, catechumens and sponsors are formally invited to enter the church and to join in the celebration of the Liturgy of the Word (*RCIA* 60). Following the homily, the catechumens should be called forward and dismissed with a book of the Gospels or a cross (*RCIA* 64). They are specially included in the Mass' intercessory prayers before being formally dismissed from the assembly in order to pray and reflect upon the Scriptures (*RCIA* 65–67).

Other Rites in the Catechumenate

Other liturgical rites during this period, although optional, are significant to the continuing faith development of both participants and parishes:

- celebrations of the word of God (*RCIA* 81–89)

- minor exorcisms (*RCIA* 90–93)

- blessings (*RCIA* 95–96)

- anointing (*RCIA* 98–101)

- sending (*RCIA* 106–17).

Rite of Election

The importance of this rite is accented by the fact that it is often celebrated by the bishop (or bishop's representative) at the diocesan cathedral. The transition is marked further by a change of title and in the selection of the godparent(s) beforehand.

After the catechumens have been presented to the bishop and approved by the assembly (*RCIA* 130–31), their names are inscribed in the *Book of the Elect* (*RCIA* 132). Intercessory prayers and a special blessing for the elect follow this sacred moment.

The Scrutinies

1. The first scrutiny takes place on the third Sunday of Lent. Its focus is the story of the Samaritan woman at the well (John 4:5–42). After special intercessory prayers, the celebrant prays that the elect may be exorcised from the powers of sin (RCIA 150–156). During the week that follows, the presentation of the Creed should be formally made, preferably after a homily within Mass (RCIA 157–163).

2. The second scrutiny takes place on the fourth Sunday of Lent. It focuses on the story of the man born blind (John 9:1–41). Again, after the intercessions, the celebrant prays that the elect may be exorcised from the powers of sin (RCIA 164–70).

3. The fifth Sunday of Lent brings the third scrutiny. This Sunday focuses on the raising of Lazarus (John 11:1–45). Intercessory prayers from the worshiping community and prayers of exorcism from the celebrant again follow (RCIA 171–77). During the following week, the presentation of the Lord's Prayer should be made, preferably after the reading of the Lord's Prayer from Matthew's Gospel. Following the homily, the celebrant calls on the community to silently pray for the elect. Before they are dismissed, the celebrant bestows a special blessing upon the elect (RCIA 178–84).

Rites of Preparation

When it's possible to bring the elect together on Holy Saturday for reflection and prayer, these rites may be used in immediate preparation for the reception of the sacraments (*RCIA* 185 and following). If the *presentation of the Creed* or the *presentation of the Lord's Prayer* has not been celebrated already, they could be celebrated now. An *ephphetha rite* (a rite of opening the ears and mouth, symbolizing the hearing and proclaiming of the word) is a fitting preparation rite, as is the rite of *choosing a baptismal name*. Any or all of these rites serve to set the stage for the highlight of the RCIA experience: the sacraments of initiation.

Sacraments of Initiation

After months or years of sharing the faith, the RCIA journey culminates in this very special parish celebration. Holy Saturday is the night to celebrate, and the Church celebrates in style. In the early Church the Easter Vigil lasted until dawn; today's vigil lasts only a few hours (depending on the parish, generally between two and four). It is the most glorious celebration of the entire liturgical year.

1. This night begins in total darkness. The parish community may assemble outside for the blessing of the fire. Then, as the celebrant processes into the church proclaiming the Light of Christ, each person lights a taper from the new Easter candle that has been blessed and ignited with the new fire. Soon the church is aglow with flame.

2. The Liturgy of the Word begins in the light. Seven readings from the Old Testament are provided, but it is not necessary to proclaim all seven. In some places, the Old Testament readings are proclaimed by candlelight. Psalms are interspersed between each reading.

3. Before the New Testament epistle is read, the *Gloria* rings out, the altar candles are lit, and the Church bells are joyously rung. With this, the glorious *Alleluia*, the Gospel, and the homily, the stage is set for the sacraments of initiation.

4. The rite of baptism begins with the calling forth of those to be baptized. A litany of the saints follows, and the celebrant blesses the water by plunging the Easter candle into the baptismal pool. Baptism follows, and the newly baptized are clothed in white garments.

5. Once the baptisms are concluded, the candidates are called forward to profess their belief in the holy Catholic Church. They join the newly baptized, and the rite of confirmation is celebrated with the laying on of hands and anointing with chrism. Then the whole assembly renews their baptismal vows and the celebrant ritually sprinkles everyone with the newly blessed waters of baptism.

6. The Mass continues with the Universal Prayer and the Liturgy of the Eucharist. When it's time to receive Communion, the new Catholics—along with their godparents, sponsors, catechists, and family members—lead the congregation in the eucharistic feast. This is the culmination of initiation: sharing at the table and being sent forth.

Traits of an Effective RCIA Team Member or Catechist

You don't have to be a theology professor or an experienced minister to be a successful catechist. Certain traits and techniques can make the process of faith formation easier and more enjoyable.

- **Meet regularly throughout the process.** Several weeks before the start of a new program or upon the arrival of a new inquirer, review the materials and determine where and when to hold the sessions. Good planning ensures that the process goes smoothly.

- **Be flexible.** Resist the temptation to create a precise schedule. Remain open to the workings of the Spirit in those who present themselves. Each session should include an opportunity for unfinished or previous business to be addressed. Often questions come up between sessions that were not apparent during your time together.

- **Make each team member aware of the topics discussed**, materials covered, and questions raised in each session so there will be continuity among sessions and presenters. Contact the next session's presenters and brief them on any issues that surfaced or may need to be addressed.

- **Link your presentations and discussions to their life experience**. Catechists and team members are also learners, catalysts, and partners—not directors. Share stories the children can relate to and use uncomplicated language without talking down to the children in your class.

- **Be attentive and receptive**. Communication, especially active listening, is one of your greatest tools in establishing trust. Look at the person and give him or her your undivided attention. Try to hear and be open to what is said. Let each child in your class know you care.

- **Practice empathy and sensitivity**. This requires a compassionate attitude and an awareness of your reactions and prejudices. Accept and affirm the uniqueness of each individual and genuinely desire to feel *with* her or him. The rest of the group will follow your example. Create a safe space for the children to explore their faith. Never isolate a child or make one feel as though her or his thoughts or questions are abnormal. If a child is difficult or disruptive in class, approach the individual alone and be compassionate but firm. If necessary, meet with his or her parents to discuss your concerns.

- **Take advantage of opportunities for renewal and training**. Faith is a relationship. While routines and habits are helpful, don't live by a script. Remain open to the opportunities and creative diversions of the Spirit. Above all, make time for your own spiritual growth. Take time daily for prayer. Practice the faith you share. Grow in Christ. Stay informed on new teachings and trends in the Church. Attend retreats and seminars and read books that develop your understanding and ministry skills. Be as present in the sacraments and active in the life of the parish as you hope your catechumens and candidates will be.

- **Form a hospitality team**. This team will provide snacks and beverages at each session and a well-planned and generously provided menu for the Easter Vigil retreat. This team does not need to stay for the sessions. In fact, they may wish to remain anonymous until the retreat, which becomes an opportunity for team members to reveal themselves and Christ's love in action.

- **Establish an intercessory team**. Have parishioners sign up to become a prayer partner (a secret intercessor who promises to pray for a particular catechumen or candidate throughout the RCIA process). If your parish has a parish school or youth group, encourage older children or teens to be prayer partners with the children in your group. The children will be encouraged to be active in their new faith if they see their peers and peer-mentors actively practicing their faith, too!

Traits of an Effective RCIA Sponsor

There is no one way to be a good sponsor, but certain qualities do increase a sponsor's potential. These qualities will help you recruit, maintain, and even *be* a better sponsor:

- *A sponsor is willing to share the faith*. A sponsor should talk with his or her catechumen about his or her faith, love, commitment, and relationship with Jesus Christ. This person shares simple ways to put our faith into words and actions to help the catechumen deepen his or her relationship with Jesus.

- *A sponsor is prayerful*. A sponsor has and knows the importance of an active prayer life and prays for his or her catechumen. This person is aware of and sensitive to the many different ways of praying. He or she may even teach the catechumen how to pray.

- *A sponsor is welcoming and hospitable*. A good sponsor makes her or his catechumen feel comfortable in and around the parish. Whether at an RCIA session, Mass, or another parish function, this person makes a special effort to greet the catechumen, sit and visit with him or her, and introduce her or him to others.

- *A sponsor is a good listener*. All catechumens seek God in one way or another. Some are very forthcoming with their story and questions, others are more reluctant. Sometimes what is *not* said is revealing. A good sponsor remains available, respects privacy, and listens as much—if not more—than he or she talks.

- *A sponsor is understanding and supportive*. A sponsor tries to understand the catechumen's feelings, concerns, joys, and uncertainties. This person shows empathy and compassion no matter what is going on and how the person feels. This person should also establish an open line of communication with the catechumen's parents. As the children go through the RCIA, it is important for them to have the support not only of their sponsor but of their parents. If something serious arises, he or she can refer the catechumen to the RCIA coordinator or pastor.

- *A sponsor is informed and involved*. Good sponsors help their catechumen by staying informed of news and events not only in the parish and the RCIA but also in the larger and universal Church. This person reads the bulletin, follows the Church in the media, and keeps track of the RCIA schedule. Better yet, he or she attends every session possible and obtains copies of the material to share in the experience and renew her or his own understanding.

- *A sponsor is willing to challenge*. If a catechumen shows a lack of commitment, serious hesitation, or resistance to the process, the sponsor should ask kindly about the situation. Being honest and willing to talk about potential conflicts will ensure the spiritual well-being and best interests of the catechumen and the Church. The RCIA coordinator or pastor may know the best way to address difficult situations.

Integrating the Parish Community

The RCIA process can renew the entire parish. It is a constant reminder of our roots, our heritage, and our traditions. Each beginning offers an opportunity for all to revisit their own journey of faith, to share how God is with us, and to mature in our relationships with God and each other. When expressed through the life of the parish, the RCIA can facilitate a continuous conversion process throughout the community and a clearer image of the reign of God.

- Provide RCIA updates for the parish bulletin, newsletter, or website, sharing ways parishioners can help the group and introducing them to the names and faces of the participants (see also hospitality and intercessory teams above).

- Post the first names of catechumens and candidates in the adoration chapel to remind visitors to intercede for RCIA participants.

- As you approach the rite of election, post photos of the RCIA participants in the vestibule or narthex of the church to remind the parish to welcome and pray for the group. When working with children, you will need parental consent before posting any photos of children in public places. If you are unable to share photos, a photo of your empty classroom with a reminder to pray for the group works, too.

- Invite parish groups and committees to send an encouraging letter to the group. These could include an introduction to their membership or ministry as well as a special gift:

  o A men's or women's group might provide journals or writing utensils.

  o The rosary group might send rosaries for the lesson on Catholic prayers and practices.

  o The fish friers or food-pantry volunteers might provide snacks for each session.

  o The altar guild or maintenance crew might deliver flowers for the room each month.

  o The parish school or youth group could design cards or bookmarks for children going through the RCIA. Or ask high school students in your parish to "buddy" with a child in your group and send him or her an RCIA "care" package.

Discerning Individual Needs

No one can predict the makeup of an RCIA group. The variety of ages, backgrounds, and catechetical needs within any group, year, or parish can be huge.

Religious Heritage and Formation Level

Participants will come to you from a variety of faith backgrounds. Some may have had no faith formation or have little, if any, concept of Church, faith, and salvation. Others may have inherited biases against certain Church teachings. You may have someone who was baptized and active in another Christian denomination and someone who was baptized Catholic but not raised in the Church.

While catechumens and candidates can usually participate in the sessions together, the lived experiences of an active Christian and the experiences of someone without any faith background make for very different perspectives. In the celebration of the rites, the reality of baptism must be evidenced, so during the rites these two groups may need to be separated as a way of addressing their separate needs and backgrounds. Effective entrance questions and strong communications among the RCIA leaders, sponsors, and pastor should prevent critical surprises and lead each participant to initiation or full reception into the universal Church.

Be careful to avoid generating a one-size-fits-all process. As you prepare for each session, cater the discussions, questions, and activities to each group's needs. If you anticipate a strong interest in a subject or benefit to highlighting certain aspects of Catholic teaching or practice, do so with prudence, charity, and guidance from your pastor.

Personal Commitments and Situations

Some children come to the RCIA process with a strong desire to learn about the Catholic faith and others may participate out of insistence from their parents or other outside sources. Some children may struggle with the process or in understanding Church teaching beyond more rules they have to follow. Others may face obstacles to regular attendance or full participation—an overabundance of extracurriculars or schoolwork, limited access to transportation, medical or physical challenges, or irregular family situations. Here your loving response is essential in guiding each participant in his or her faith journey. Before a child begins the RCIA process, make sure to meet his or her parents and get to know what kind of additional help or encouragement the child might need to be successful.

Each participant has human dignity and is created in the image of God. Most of us have been affected by sin, whether our own or that of others, but all of us are called to conversion and new life. Use the RCIA process and other parish resources to provide the time, support, and environment each participant requires.

How to Use *Journey of Faith*

Journey of Faith consists of:

- *Forty-eight* catechetical lessons.

- *Three Leader Guides* for each age group: *Inquiry*, *Catechumenate*, and *Enlightenment and Mystagogy*.

Catechetical Lessons (Handouts)

Journey of Faith is presented in forty-eight personal, engaging, and manageable lessons so that uncatechized or nominally catechized children can hear the good news. The lessons are divided according to the four periods of initiation:

- Sixteen **Inquiry** (Q#) lessons broadly cover basic questions in areas such as: what is faith, revelation, prayer, the Bible, and the meaning of the Mass and Catholic practices.

- Sixteen **Catechumenate** (C#) lessons address more catechetical aspects of our faith: the Church, the sacraments, the moral life, and more.

- Eight **Enlightenment** (E#) lessons focus on preparing the elect for the various rites, especially the sacraments of initiation, and guide them through Lenten themes and events.

- Eight **Mystagogy** (M#) lessons redirect the focus of new Catholics from learning to living.

In each lesson you will find:

- an introductory illustration and story to apply the topic to something the children can relate to.

- an explanation of a faith topic.

- related Scripture and *Catechism* references.

- questions for reflection and discussion.

- interactive activities throughout the lesson to keep the children engaged.

- integrated images, icons, and sidebars throughout the program.

- a final wrap-up activity to reinforce the lesson objectives.

- "In Short": a brief list of statements summarizing the key points of the lesson.

The tables of contents and following schedules provide an effective and logical order for a typical parish-based RCIA process. Because the topics and themes are closely connected and recur throughout the *Journey of Faith* program and liturgical year, the handouts and *Leader Guides* can serve as ongoing tools. We understand that time is limited and that questions and issues arise. Ultimately, how you use the material depends on you, your parish, and the needs of each participant. Both the handouts and the *Leader Guides* are designed to walk you through the sessions and facilitate discussions, highlighting and reinforcing essential points along the way.

Leader Guides

To help you present each topic and prepare for the sessions, each *Journey of Faith Leader Guide* provides a lesson plan for each catechetical handout within its respective period and an alphabetical glossary of terms contained in those lessons. When used sequentially as a set, this creates a comprehensive RCIA program that is adaptable to any parish and group of participants. Along with the schedules and supply lists in this *Inquiry Leader Guide*, *Journey of Faith* equips RCIA leaders to engage participants and their sponsors in the process of conversion and faith formation.

Each lesson plan is designed to fill a session lasting forty-five to sixty minutes, not including any liturgical celebrations. As session times may vary, the material in each lesson plan can be adapted to your specific needs. Continuously assess your participants' understanding and tailor your presentation to what the group needs. Depending on the age of the children in your group, it may be difficult for them to concentrate for the entire allotted time, especially if classes are after school. Try to schedule breaks or active, kinesthetic activities so the children have a chance to release excess energy.

In addition to the complete participant lesson, leaders will find instructions, background information, notes, and more under these headings:

Catechism	sections of the *Catechism of the Catholic Church* covered by that lesson, plus a key quote selected from the list.
Objectives	learning goals; what participants should know and be able to do after the session.
Leader Meditation	brief reflections, questions, and prayers on a Scripture passage related to the lesson's topic.
Leader Preparation	tips and reminders to guide the presenter's preparation for the session, including a list of that lesson's vocabulary and special supplies.
Welcome	reminders and ideas for the beginning of a session, whether transitioning from a Liturgy of the Word or settling the group in.
Opening Scripture	a reading from Scripture that sets the context and supports the lesson's topic, followed by a transition question.
Discussion of Lesson Handout	points, prompts, and additional lesson notes and references for the leader organized by section.
Activities	instructions and suggested responses for all activities in the lesson.
Closing Prayer	prompts or texts to end the session in prayer.
Take-Home	exercises that participants complete between sessions either by themselves or with the rest of their families to deepen and apply their formation. Leaders should instruct participants before each departure and follow up as needed.

Leader Meditations: Preparing With Scripture

Before each session, catechists and team members should read the Scripture passage for that lesson as well as review the lesson plan and any accompanying catechetical material. As you reflect on the passage, consider these questions:

- Become part of the narrative. What stories of your own faith journey come to mind?

- What questions are raised in your mind?

- What are the sights, sounds, and feelings that emerge?

- What are the names and stories of the key individuals?

- What are the connections, if any, between the passage and the lesson's topic? Between the passage and other Bible readings, especially those for Sunday Mass?

- How does this passage apply to today's Church and Christian living?

- If you have time, read a devotion or commentary on the passage to deepen your understanding.

If needed, adjust the session's timing or focus to maximize your catechumens' and candidates' success with the material. After your lesson is set, relax and enjoy the opportunity to share your faith with those who are eager to be touched by God's Spirit.

More Resources

Liguori Publications offers many resources for RCIA leaders and participants, including DVDs, pamphlets, and electronic publications. Always explain the purpose of any supplemental material and leave time in the sessions to share reactions and findings.

Visit Liguori.org for our full and latest offerings and ordering details. Be sure to purchase copies well in advance of the scheduled sessions. Ordering enough for the entire parish builds a community connection to the RCIA and a foundation for ongoing catechesis.

No matter how far in advance you plan your purchase, unexpected things come up. Whether it's a new volunteer to your RCIA team or a new family of participants, these last-minute changes can leave you in a bind. You know photocopying material violates the copyright, but what do you do when you only have a few days or hours to find a solution? Liguori can help you out in these kinds of emergencies through rush delivery or even short-term permission to duplicate material while you wait for your order to arrive. To find out how we can help, call us call at 1-800-325-9521 or email us at Liguori@Liguori.org.

Practical Suggestions

Materials and Supplies

The leader preparation tips suggest helpful items specific to each lesson. For most sessions, you will need the following:

- a complete set of *Journey of Faith* handouts for each participant (it's best to buy additional sets for sponsors).

- copies of the *Journey of Faith Leader Guides* for each catechist and team member.

- multiple, ideally individual, copies of the Holy Bible. (*Journey of Faith* uses the *New American Bible,* revised edition.)

- multiple, ideally individual, copies of the *Catechism of the Catholic Church (CCC).*

- a Bible concordance to help leaders locate related passages (optional).

- a simple white candle in a secure holder.

- matches or a lighter.

- nametags for the first few sessions.

- comfortable seating for each individual positioned near tables or other writing/ working surfaces.

- pens, pencils, and notebooks or paper.

Journaling and Notes

Like the faith journey, the reflection and writing process can be highly personal. Some write more than others or prefer certain mediums and styles. The handouts offer limited writing space for questions, Bible references, and activities. However, keeping an RCIA journal fulfills a number of purposes:

- recalling thoughts and reactions to the topics, readings, and discussions.

- writing longer responses to the questions and activities.

- jotting down notes and questions during and beyond the sessions.

- recording insights, ideas, and feelings throughout the RCIA process.

At the first session, provide participants with a journal, or if they prefer, they may bring their own. Encourage them to use it every week and to spend time in personal reflection. Let them know they are not required to share anything private with the group or with their sponsor.

Preparing a Sacred Space

Scripture reading, faith discussions, and prayer require reverence. Your environment sets the tone for each session and much of the process. Make sure the room has an inviting atmosphere. Modifying the space to match the session's topic, RCIA period, or liturgical season will assist the participants as they move through the process and grow in their familiarity with Catholic culture, ethos, and identity. You may also want to pray with the group for the Holy Spirit to be with you as you begin your opening Scripture each session to better prepare the hearts and minds of participants and you as a leader.

- Reverently lay the Bible or *Lectionary* next to the candle. During each of the sacred seasons, place liturgically colored fabric underneath: **green** during Ordinary Time, **violet** during Advent and Lent, and **white** during Christmas and Easter.

- Add religious images and objects to the space.

- Appeal to all of the participants' senses. Consider playing sacred music as they enter the space or meditative sounds as they pray or write in their journals. Encourage anyone who provides refreshments to be creative and to match the snack to the topic, season, or a saint whose feast lands on or near the session date.

In the Beginning: The First Few Sessions

1. Warmly welcome the participants, sponsors, and guests. Encourage sponsors to attend every session with their participant, and invite parents to sit in if they're able.

2. Have each child introduce himself or herself. Ask each one to briefly explain what led him or her to inquire about the Catholic faith or accept a supporting role in the RCIA.

3. Distribute the materials, state your expectations for the program, and give any instructions or announcements, such as directions to the restrooms.

4. Explain the purpose and meaning of the sessions. Uncatechized children may be unfamiliar with prayer, candlelighting, Scripture reading and reflection, faith sharing, or religious instruction—especially in a Catholic setting.

5. Whenever reading from Scripture, make sure the reader is comfortable with reading aloud and understands the passage. Scripture should be proclaimed prayerfully and clearly and, if possible, with prior preparation. Never oblige anyone, but invite all interested to receive guidance from a practiced leader or minister.

6. Always model the behavior and etiquette desired, whether at Mass or in the sessions. While gentle reminders are needed at times, people of all ages learn from example.

7. Allow time before, after, or outside the sessions for fellowship, socializing, and refreshments. This allows the personal connections and private conversations essential for spiritual growth to take place.

Answering Questions

Most participants enter the RCIA process with religious or spiritual questions as well as preconceived notions of the Catholic Church. More questions will undoubtedly emerge as they near initiation. Furthermore, the time they spend in the sessions and even with the parish community will not completely encompass their experience and knowledge of faith. Catechists and team members must be willing to engage tough questions and events in order to further the individual's understanding and conversion.

Always respect every question and respond to it as adequately as you can, especially if it is pertinent to the topic and the entire group. Never attempt to answer a question that goes beyond your knowledge or expertise.

If you don't feel qualified or aren't sure how to answer:

- Let the child know you need time to prepare a proper or fuller answer. Offer to respond at the next session or outside of the sessions, and follow through.

- Check trusted and authoritative sources for relevant Church teachings and key factors in your response. Share your references or recommend similar material when the question is revisited.

- Consult with your director or coordinator of religious education, pastor, or diocesan official, or set up a private conversation between that contact and the person to answer the question more thoroughly.

If an individual query or a barrage of questions draws the discussion away from the topic at hand, consider dedicating a portion or an entire session to the subject of interest.

RCIA Schedules Using *Journey of Faith*

Program or Academic Year
(Fall–Pentecost)

The following guidelines direct parishes in scheduling an RCIA program lasting eight to nine months each year. Weekly schedules may vary from year to year depending on when Advent, Lent, and the rites occur. Merging or separating lessons into adjacent weeks will keep you on track and maximize the program's connection to liturgical feasts and themes.

Journey of Faith strongly recommends continuing after Easter into a discrete period of mystagogy. This provides the parish an additional opportunity to join the neophytes and witness to the value of, and universal call to, ongoing faith formation.

Three Months Before Advent (August–September)		
First Week	Q1	"Welcome to the RCIA!"
Second Week	Q2	"What Is Faith?"
Third Week	Q3	"Trinity: Three in One"
Fourth Week	Q4	"Who Is Jesus Christ?"

Two Months Before Advent (September–October)		
First Week	Q5	"The Bible"
	Q6	"Where We Find God"
Second Week	Q7	"Your Prayer Life"
	Q8	"Catholic Prayers"
Third Week	Q9	"The Mass"
	C5	"The Sacrament of the Eucharist"
Fourth Week	Q10	"The Church Year"
	Q11	"Places in a Catholic Church"

One Month Before Advent (October–November)		
First Week	Q12	"Who Shepherds the Church?"
	Q13	"The Church as Community"
Second Week/ All Saints	Q14	"Mary"
	Q15	"The Saints"
Third Week	Q16	"What's Life After Death?"
Fourth Week/ Christ the King	C1	"RCIA Process and Rites" (*anticipates rites of acceptance and welcoming*)

Advent and Christmas (November–December)		
First Week	C10	"The People of God"
Second Week	C11	"The Early Church"
	C12	"Church History"
Third Week	C2	"The Sacraments: An Introduction"
Fourth Week/ Christmas		BREAK
Holy Family/ Epiphany	C8	"The Sacrament of Matrimony"
	C9	"The Sacrament of Holy Orders"
Baptism of the Lord (OT)	C3	"The Sacrament of Baptism"
	C4	"The Sacrament of Confirmation"

One Month Before Lent (January–February)		
First Week	C6	"The Sacrament of Penance and Reconciliation"
	C7	"The Sacrament of the Anointing of the Sick"
Second Week	C13	"Living Like Jesus Today"
	C14	"Caring for All God's Creatures"
Third Week	C15	"Choose Life Always"
	C16	"Caring for God's Community"
Week of Ash Wednesday	E1	"Election: Saying 'Yes' to Jesus" (*anticipates rite of election*)

Lent/Enlightenment (February–March)		
First Week	E2	"Living Lent"
Second Week	E3	"Reflecting on Our Choices"
	E4	"The Creed" (anticipates third Sunday)
Third Week	E5	"The Way of the Cross"
Fourth Week	E6	"The Lord's Prayer" (anticipates fifth Sunday)
Fifth Week	E7	"The Meaning of Holy Week"
Holy Week	E8	"Easter Vigil Retreat"

Easter/Mystagogy (April–May)		
First Week		BREAK (or appropriate fellowship)
Second Week	M1	"Our Faith Is a Lifelong Process"
Third Week	M2	"The Role of the Laity"
	M7	"Family Life"
Fourth Week	M3	"Your Spiritual Gifts"
Fifth Week	M4	"Making Tough Decisions"
Sixth Week/ Ascension	M5	"Our Call to Holiness"
	M6	"Living the Virtues"
Seventh Week/ Pentecost (Final Session)	M8	"Sharing the Good News"

Calendar Year (ongoing, sequential)

The forty-eight *Journey of Faith* lessons can be followed sequentially with only minor adjustments for the rites and the Lenten season. Using this model, parishes would begin about *four weeks after Pentecost*. To complete the calendar year, we recommend a single-week break for Christmas and Easter and a two-week break shortly after Pentecost for program renewal, training, and family time. Refer to the *Journey of Faith* contents pages for the full sequence.

Liturgical Year (ongoing, nonsequential)

For parishes following the ongoing catechumenal model, each phase in the RCIA process is available all year long. We recommend using separate but simultaneous tracks for inquiry and catechumenate and a third track during Lent and Easter. In this way, the process is open and flexible enough to support and honor the needs and pace of each catechumen and candidate.

In this model, most individuals will spend a year or more in the RCIA process. The lessons will be used as they relate to the themes of each Sunday's readings. A suggested outline of how the forty-eight lessons can be applied to Sunday readings can be found in each volume of *The Word Into Life*, though for children's formation this is recommended to guide the leader only. The material in *The Word Into Life* is written for adult participants.

My RCIA Schedule

This chart can be reused or adjusted each year according to your parish's RCIA calendar. It is also valuable for participants who may be on a separate path from the rest of the group. Make sure to record all key dates and details and to follow your RCIA director's or pastor's instructions.

Parish: _____

Pastor/RCIA Director: _____

Catechist(s)/
Team Member(s): _____

Participant(s): _____

_____

_____

_____

_____

_____

_____

_____

_____

_____

_____

_____

Class Time(s): _____

Class Location: _____

Mass Time: _____

Easter Vigil: _____

INQUIRY			
Lesson Title	Session Date	Lesson Title	Session Date
Q1: "Welcome to the RCIA!"		Q9: "The Mass"	
Q2: "What Is Faith?"		Q10: "The Church Year"	
Q3: "Trinity: Three in One"		Q11: "Places in a Catholic Church"	
Q4: "Who Is Jesus Christ?"		Q12: "Who Shepherds the Church?"	
Q5: "The Bible"		Q13: "The Church as Community"	
Q6: "Where We Find God"		Q14: "Mary"	
Q7: "Your Prayer Life"		Q15: "The Saints"	
Q8: "Catholic Prayers"		Q16: "What's Life After Death?"	

CATECHUMENATE

Lesson Title	Session Date	Lesson Title	Session Date
C1: "The RCIA Process and Rites"		C9: "The Sacrament of Holy Orders"	
C2: "The Sacraments: An Introduction"		C10: "The People of God"	
C3: "The Sacrament of Baptism"		C11: "The Early Church"	
C4: "The Sacrament of Confirmation"		C12: "Church History"	
C5: "The Sacrament of the Eucharist"		C13: "Living Like Jesus Today"	
C6: "The Sacrament of Penance and Reconciliation"		C14: "Caring for All God's Creatures"	
C7: "The Sacrament of the Anointing of the Sick"		C15: "Choose Life Always"	
C8: "The Sacrament of Matrimony"		C16: "Caring for God's Community"	

ENLIGHTENMENT / MYSTAGOGY

Lesson Title	Session Date	Lesson Title	Session Date
E1: "Saying 'Yes' to Jesus"		M1: "Our Faith Is a Lifelong Process"	
E2: "Living Lent"		M2: "The Role of the Laity"	
E3: "Reflecting on Our Choices"		M3: "Your Spiritual Gifts"	
E4: "The Creed"		M4: "Making Tough Decisions"	
E5: "The Way of the Cross"		M5: "Our Call to Holiness"	
E6: "The Lord's Prayer"		M6: "Living the Virtues"	
E7: "The Meaning of Holy Week"		M7: "Family Life"	
E8: "Easter Vigil Retreat"		M8: "Sharing the Good News"	

Q1: Welcome to the RCIA

Catechism: 1229–49

Objectives

- Describe the RCIA as a time to ask questions about the faith.
- List the four phases, or periods, of the RCIA.
- Identify the RCIA as rooted in early Christian history.

Leader Meditation

Psalm 139:1–16

Think about your own faith journey. Consider the many times God has protected and guided you. Now, consider the ones this same God has entrusted to your care. Imagine the trust God has in you. You have been given the opportunity to be their companion and guide on their faith journey. Pray for wisdom and courage. Rely on the Lord's help.

Leader Preparation

- Read the lesson handout, this lesson plan, the Scripture passage, and the *Catechism* sections.
- Read the front sections of this *Leader Guide*. Publications on usccb.org may also help you explain the RCIA and the *Catechism* further.
- Gather copies of the *New American Bible* and the *Catechism* for each participant as well as any required materials. Enlist creative ways to supply prayer journals and other unique items.
- Be familiar with the vocabulary terms for this lesson: catechist, *Catechism of the Catholic Church*, Rite of Christian Initiation of Adults, rite, initiation, catechumen, candidate, inquiry, catechumenate, godparent, sponsor, purification and enlightenment, sacraments of initiation, sacraments, baptism, Communion, confirmation, mystagogy. Definitions can be found in this guide's glossary.

Welcome

Greet the children as they arrive. Check for supplies and immediate needs. Solicit questions or comments about the previous lesson and/or share new information and findings. Begin promptly.

Opening Scripture

Psalm 139:1–16

If any of the children in your group are unfamiliar with the Bible, briefly review its organization and how to look up readings before you begin (you will probably have to do this multiple times before the children get familiar with how to do it). Light the candle and explain that it is a sign and a reminder of the Lord's presence.

After reading the selection, ask the children what the Psalm made them think of as they were listening to it. Share a few words of encouragement and affirmation. Let the children know that God is leading them and has been with them from the beginning.

> God…reveals himself and gives himself to man, at the same time bringing man a superabundant light as he searches for the ultimate meaning of his life.
>
> CCC 26

Journey of Faith

Welcome to the RCIA

It was the first day of RCIA class. Tanya, Terrence, Tomás, and Lisa didn't know what to expect.

"Hello!" Mrs. and Mr. Evans, their teachers, greeted them by the door.

"Hi," everyone replied shyly.

"Let's all get to know each other," said Mrs. Evans, smiling. "Who wants to share why they're here?"

"My mom told me I had to," Tomás said, chuckling.

"I don't know," Tanya said, shrugging.

"It has to do with being Catholic," Lisa replied.

Welcome to the RCIA

- Read this section with your group or ask for a volunteer to do so who feels comfortable reading by himself or herself. Then ask your group if anyone feels like Tomás (they're in RCIA because their parents told them they had to), or like Tanya (they aren't really sure why they're here), or like Lisa (they know it has something to do with becoming Catholic).

- Then ask for volunteers to share why they are in the RCIA today. If you have time, you can turn this into an icebreaker activity by going around the room and asking the children to share their name, why they're here, what school they go to, and an interesting fact about themselves.

- Continue reading (or have a volunteer read) the next part of the story.

- Pause to show the children a copy of the *Catechism of the Catholic Church*, pass a copy around, or, if you have a copy for each child in your class, hand them out.

- Finish the section and ask the children if they will be candidates or catechumens. If you gave the children nametags (or had them decorate their own), ask the children to write "candidate" or "catechumen" under their name.

Mr. Evans nodded and said, "It does. By the end of class you'll all know exactly why you're here. And what RCIA has to do with being Catholic."

Why are you in RCIA today?

Mr. Evans continued. "Mrs. Evans and I are your catechists. A **catechist** is someone who teaches you about religion using a book called a catechism. We'll use a book called the ***Catechism of the Catholic Church*** since you're here to learn about being Catholic." Mr. Evans held up a huge book.

"We're not going to have to learn *all* that, are we?" Terrence asked. He looked shocked.

"No," Mr. Evans said, laughing. "That would be a lot! This class is just the beginning."

"Are these classes just for kids?" Tanya asked.

"Yes and no," said Mrs. Evans. "These classes are just for you. The process you're going through is for kids your age, teenagers, and adults. It's called the **Rite of Christian Initiation of Adults**, or RCIA for short."

Lisa frowned and said, "But we're not adults."

"Actually, you are to the Church. The Catholic Church says people are adults if they can think for themselves and tell right from wrong or good from bad. Then you can decide to be Catholic. It's a big decision. That's why we have these classes. They get you ready for the rite."

"What's a rite?" Tanya asked.

"A **rite** is a serious religious ceremony," Mrs. Evans said. "This rite is Christian. That means it's

connected to Jesus Christ. The early Church used something a lot like this to initiate new Christians, too. Does anyone know what initiation means?"

"**Initiation** means to start something or what you go through to become part of a group," Lisa answered.

"Good!" Mrs. Evans said. "Right now, you're all thinking about becoming Catholic. But you're all coming from different places. Some of you have been to church before. Some of you went to a different church.

"Some of you were baptized when you were babies. Some of you are getting baptized when you become Catholic. If you're going to be baptized, you're called a **catechumen**. If you've already been baptized as a Christian, you'll be called a **candidate**."

"But no matter what you're called," Mr. Evans added, "you're all still working together."

Will you be a catechumen or a candidate?

"You'll all go through four stages. The first one is called **inquiry**. To inquire means to ask questions. In this stage you get to ask questions about God and being Catholic. But don't worry! You can still have questions after inquiry.

"The second stage is called **catechumenate**. You'll learn about most of the major Catholic beliefs. You'll also find someone to help you on your journey. That person is called a **godparent** if you haven't been baptized. If you have, the person is a **sponsor**. This person can be a family member or a friend, but the person has to be a confirmed Catholic."

"What does a sponsor or godparent do?" asked Tanya.

"They're like your personal guide. You can ask them questions or talk to them about being Catholic when you aren't in class. They also make sure you take what we learn in class and use it every day.

"The third stage is called **purification and enlightenment**. This happens during Lent. What do you know about Lent?"

"My grandma says Lent is when we get ready for Easter," Tomás answered.

"Good! You will be getting ready for Easter. You'll also be getting ready to become fully Catholic. You clean up, or purify, the things that keep you from God. You also learn about God, God's love, and how to make God happy. That makes you enlightened."

"That sounds like a lot of work," Terrence said. "Why do we do all that?"

"Well, on the night before Easter, at a special Mass called the Easter Vigil, you receive the three **sacraments of initiation**: Baptism, Confirmation, and Communion. But you can't get a gift from someone you don't know. So you have to know God and invite him into your life first."

"So a sacrament is a present?"

"They certainly are a gift! **Sacraments** are visible, physical ways that we know God is with us even when we can't see him. **Baptism** takes away our sins and makes us members of the Church. **Communion**, also called the holy Eucharist, is when we receive the true Body and Blood of Jesus Christ. **Confirmation** is when the Holy Spirit comes to each of us in a special way. In some parishes you have to wait until you're a little older to be confirmed, but here you'll be confirmed along with the teenagers and adults. Does that make sense?"

Terrence nodded and said, "Kind of."

"Don't worry. It is complicated. That's why we'll discuss all seven sacraments one at a time. When the Easter Vigil gets here, you'll know everything you need to know."

"Just one more stage! After Easter, you'll start a stage called **mystagogy**. That means 'interpretation of mystery,' and we'll be uncovering even more about the mysteries of the sacraments, God's love for us, and how we can live our faith every day."

Which part of the RCIA is most exciting to you?

"We have a lot to learn," Mrs. Evans said, "so let's start at the very beginning. When you hear the word *Catholic*, what do you think of?"

Tomás had his hand up first. "I think of my grandma."

"I think of religion," said Lisa.

"Is the pope Catholic?" Tanya asked.

"Those are all good places to start," Mrs. Evans said. "Catholicism is a religion. That means all Catholics around the world share the same traditions, rituals, prayers, and set of beliefs. Catholics practice their religion by praying, going to Mass, celebrating the seven sacraments, reading the Bible and many other things. You'll learn more about all those things later.

"And you're right, Tanya, the pope is Catholic. In fact, the pope is the leader of the whole Church.

What do you think of when you hear the word Catholic?

"Before we leave, I just want to let you know that asking questions in this class is very important. So if you ever don't understand something, just ask! Does anyone have any questions before we go?"

"Is being Catholic better than being in other religions?" Tanya asked.

Tomás questioned, "Do kids have to be Catholic if their parents are?"

"What happens if I don't believe in something you teach us? Does that mean I can't be a Catholic?" Lisa wondered out loud.

• As you read about the different periods and events that occur throughout the RCIA process, ask the children if there's anything they're looking forward to. Encourage the children to be excited about the RCIA process. While the RCIA can be a lot of work, it's also an exciting time!

• Ask the group: "What do you think of when you hear the word *Catholic*?" If you have time, ask each child to come up and write down a word, place, or person they think is Catholic on a board or large sheet of paper.

Final Activity

- As you finish the lesson, ask the children if they have any questions about being Catholic.

- You may not be able to answer all their questions today, so ask the children to write their questions on an index card to hand to you as they leave. Look through these questions and see if there are any repeated questions or questions that won't be covered in the lessons. Be sure you find time to answer all these questions. Bring in a guest speaker if you don't feel you can accurately cover the topic.

WHAT QUESTIONS DO YOU HAVE ABOUT BEING CATHOLIC?

In Short

- RCIA is a time to ask questions about your faith.

- RCIA has four parts, or phases.

- RCIA is rooted in early Christian history.

Journey of Faith for Children, Inquiry, Q1 (826351)

Imprimi Potest: Stephen T. Rehrauer, CSsR, Provincial, Denver Province, the Redemptorists.

Imprimatur: "In accordance with CIC 827, permission to publish has been granted on May 2, 2017, by Bishop Mark S. Rivituso, Vicar General, Archdiocese of St. Louis. Permission to publish is an indication that nothing contrary to Church teaching is contained in this work. It does not imply any endorsement of the opinions expressed in the publication, nor is any liability assumed by this permission."

Journey of Faith © 2000, 2017 Liguori Publications, Liguori, MO 63057. To order, visit Liguori.org or call 800-325-9521. Liguori Publications, a nonprofit corporation, is an apostolate of the Redemptorists. To learn more about the Redemptorists, visit Redemptorists.com. All rights reserved. No part of this publication may be reproduced, distributed, stored, transmitted, or posted in any form by any means without prior written permission.

Editors of the 2017 *Journey of Faith for Children*: Theresa Nienaber Panuski and Pat Fosarelli, MD, DMin.

Design and production: Wendy Barnes, Lorena Mitre Jimenez, John Krus, and Bill Townsend. Illustrations: Jeff Albrecht.

Unless noted, Scripture texts in this work are taken from the *New American Bible*, revised edition © 2000, 1991, 1986, 1970 Confraternity of Christian Doctrine, Washington, D.C., and are used by permission of the copyright owner. All Rights Reserved. No part of the *New American Bible* may be reproduced in any form without permission in writing from the copyright owner. Excerpts from the English translation of the *Catechism of the Catholic Church* for the United States of America © 1994 United States Catholic Conference, Inc.—Libreria Editrice Vaticana; English translation of the *Catechism of the Catholic Church:* Modifications from the *Editio Typica* © 1997 United States Catholic Conference, Inc.—Libreria Editrice Vaticana. Compliant with *The Roman Missal,* Third Edition.

Printed in the United States of America. 21 20 19 18 17 / 5 4 3 2 1. Third Edition.

ISBN 978-0-7648-2635-1

Liguori
PUBLICATIONS
A Redemptorist Ministry

Closing Prayer

Close with this simple prayer. Ask the children to repeat each line after you.

Jesus, Lord of Life,
you are the true shepherd.

You care for us
as a shepherd cares for his sheep.

Continue to lead us
up and down the paths of life
and guide us to safety.

You defend us with your life,
and we are beginning
to recognize your voice.

Amen.

Take-Home

Before the next lesson, ask the children to ask a member of their family (or their godparent or sponsor if they have one) the following questions from this lesson: What excites you about being Catholic or about Catholicism? What questions do you have about the Catholic Church?

Q2: What Is Faith?

Catechism: 142–65, 302, 854

Objectives:

- Define faith as a gift from God.
- Realize faith, science, and reason can exist together.
- Explain that faith grows when we nurture and share it.

Leader Meditation

John 14:1–4

Read the Scripture passage, then think about the strength of your own faith. When you pray, do you believe your prayers are being heard? Do you trust that God is intimately involved in your life, even with all its difficulties and imperfections? Most important, do you see the face of God in the questioning, doubting, and sometimes challenging young children you teach?

Leader Preparation

- Read the lesson, this lesson plan, the Scripture passage, and the *Catechism* sections. "The Characteristics of Faith" (*CCC* 153–65) may help you to answer questions posed by your class, especially how faith relates to science.
- Be familiar with the vocabulary term for this lesson: faith. The definition can be found in this guide's glossary.

Welcome

As the children arrive, welcome any new inquirers and sponsors. Check for supplies and immediate needs. Ask for any questions or comments about the last lesson that may have come up since then. Begin promptly.

Opening Scripture

John 14:1–4

Light the candle and read aloud. Following the reading, allow a moment of silence and then welcome any comments or reactions to the words. Finally, ask for any special intentions.

Faith is a gift of God, a supernatural virtue infused by [God].   *CCC* 153

What Is Faith?

Tomás learned a lot about being Catholic from his grandma. But he still had a lot of questions. So when Mrs. Evans asked for questions before they started class, Tomás was ready!

"How do we know God's real? What does heaven look like? Why can't we see heaven? Why don't I hear Jesus when I pray? Why doesn't Jesus come visit us?"

"Slow down, Tomás!" Mrs. Evans said, laughing. "Those are great questions! In fact, they all have something to do with what we're talking about today. Faith. Who thinks they know what faith is?"

CHILDREN

CCC 142–65, 302, 854

What Is Faith?

- After the opening Scripture section, ask the children what they think faith means or what it means to have faith. If you have time, start a list on the board of words or phrases that come up repeatedly when you and the group think about faith.

• Give the children time to complete the list activity in this section. Walk around the room and see what they list. Then ask for volunteers to share the name of one person or thing from their list and why they made that choice. Use this time as an opportunity to go back to your first list by pointing out similar qualities between having faith and why children chose someone or something to believe in.

What Do You Think Faith Is?

Has anyone ever asked you, "Just trust me?" What does that mean? How do you know you can trust what your parents, friends, or teachers say? How do you know you can trust God?

Faith means having trust in someone or something. Religious faith means we trust in God, his word in the Bible, and the things the Church teaches us. When we have faith, we trust even when:

- we don't (or can't) know for sure;
- something seems mysterious or impossible;
- others don't believe.

It's easier to believe something if we can see it, hear it, or touch it ourselves. The more we learn, the more we understand. This makes our faith stronger. But faith doesn't just come from knowing things. It comes from trusting the person who shares the truth with us. When we have faith, we believe:

- the person speaking knows the truth;
- the person speaking is honest.

The most important person we can have faith in is Jesus Christ. We were created "in the image of God" (Genesis 1:27). That means God made us like him. God wants us to know him and to believe in him.

ACTIVITY

List five people or things that you believe in.

1. _____
2. _____
3. _____
4. _____
5. _____

God's Great Gift

You have faith in someone or something every day. You have faith that your bus will get you to school on time. You have faith that your teacher will grade your homework fairly. You have faith that your friends will sit with you at lunch. All this trust comes from God. God gives you faith in him, faith in Jesus Christ, and faith in the Catholic Church. Faith is God's way of saying:

- "I love you and want you to be your best."
- "I love you and will always take care of you."
- "I love you and will teach you what you need to know."
- "I love you and will share everything with you."

Faith and Jesus

We are starting a journey with Jesus. He will be your best friend, guide, and teacher. Jesus said many things about faith. Read these words from the Bible and then think about the promise Jesus is making:

- "Everything is possible to one who has faith" (Mark 9:23).
- "You have faith in God; have faith also in me" (John 14:1).

What promise is Jesus making? What is Jesus asking you to do?

ACTIVITY
FOUR WAYS TO GROW IN FAITH

1. Do Good Works

Jesus said, "Whatever you did for one of these least brothers of mine, you did for me" (Matthew 25:40). The people Jesus calls the "least" were the unpopular people. No one thought they were important or special except Jesus. Jesus asks us to treat everyone like a brother or sister. When we love people we wouldn't normally talk to or do things with, it brings us closer to Jesus.

Who can you help this week?

2. Read

Keep your Bible nearby so you can hear and speak to Jesus whenever you want. Read other good books, too, like stories of the saints or a book of prayers for children.

Do you have a favorite Bible story?

3. Pray

Spend some time with Jesus in prayer every day. You can pray with words, your thoughts, and even your feelings. Prayer is like talking to Jesus. Remember to listen to what Jesus has to say.

What would you like to tell Jesus?

4. Be a Friend

Jesus said, "As I have loved you, so you also should love one another" (John 13:34). Loving others makes us more like Jesus. When we act like a friend to others, we grow in faith.

How do you show your friends you care?

Four Ways to Grow in Faith

Go through each of the four ways as a group and keep lists on a board so the children have a visual reminder of all the ways they can grow their faith. You can even type up the list and send it to the children's parents to share at home.

1. The children can do good works by playing with a younger sibling, offering to do extra chores at home, sharing a favorite toy or game at school, or calling their grandparents to talk.

2. The children can grow faith by reading a Bible story with their family or reading another Catholic children's book on their own or with their family.

3. The children can pray by coming with their parents to Mass on Sunday, writing a letter to Jesus at the end of the day, or spending time alone talking to Jesus.

4. A child can be a friend to others by helping a classmate, holding the door for others, sharing a special food treat at lunch, or volunteering at home or in the neighborhood.

Faith and Jesus

Read each Scripture verse and answer the questions together as a group. Suggested responses have been included, though answers in your group may vary.

- Mark 9:23
  Jesus promises that anything is possible if we have faith and allow Jesus to work through us. Jesus asks us to have faith in him and trust that he can work through us.

As you discuss this point, remind the children that just because we pray for something doesn't mean Jesus will give it to us, just like our parents don't give us everything we ask for. Just because Jesus doesn't do exactly what we asked doesn't mean he isn't listening or that our faith isn't strong enough. This will be discussed more in future lessons as well.

- John 14:1
  Jesus says that he is God and that when we have faith in Jesus we will have eternal life.

Jesus is asking us to have faith in him just as we have faith in God the Father. This lesson comes right before the lesson on the Trinity, so you may need to remind the children that God the Father and Jesus, God the Son, are the same God.

LIVING WITH FAITH

Draw a line from the action (on the left) to the way it helps you grow in faith (on the right).

1. Drying the dishes

2. Going to church

3. Searching online about a holy person

4. Calling a classmate who is sad

5. Going to your aunt's birthday party

6. Asking God for help before a test

7. Helping an injured player off the field

8. Reading a Bible story

9. Giving your allowance to the poor

10. Buying your friend a birthday gift

A. Doing good works

B. Reading

C. Praying

D. Being a friend

In Short

- Faith is a gift from God.
- Faith, science, and reason exist together.
- Faith grows when we nurture and share it.

Journey of Faith for Children, Inquiry, Q2 (826351)

Imprimi Potest: Stephen T. Rehrauer, CSsR, Provincial, Denver Province, the Redemptorists.

Imprimatur: "In accordance with CIC 827, permission to publish has been granted on May 3, 2017, by Bishop Mark S. Rivituso, Vicar General, Archdiocese of St. Louis. Permission to publish is an indication that nothing contrary to Church teaching is contained in this work. It does not imply any endorsement of the opinions expressed in the publication, nor is any liability assumed by this permission."

Journey of Faith © 2000, 2017 Liguori Publications, Liguori, MO 63057. To order, visit Liguori.org or call 800-325-9521. Liguori Publications, a nonprofit corporation, is an apostolate of the Redemptorists. To learn more about the Redemptorists, visit Redemptorists.com. All rights reserved. No part of this publication may be reproduced, distributed, stored, transmitted, or posted in any form by any means without prior written permission.

Editors of the 2017 Journey of Faith for Children: Theresa Nienaber-Panuski and Pat Fosarelli, MD, DMin.

Design and production: Wendy Barnes, Lorena Mitre Jimenez, John Krus, and Bill Townsend. Illustrations: Jeff Albrecht.

Unless noted, Scripture texts in this work are taken from the New American Bible, revised edition © 2010, 1991, 1986, 1970 Confraternity of Christian Doctrine, Washington, D.C., and are used by permission of the copyright owner. All Rights Reserved. No part of the New American Bible may be reproduced in any form without permission in writing from the copyright owner. Excerpts from the English translation of the Catechism of the Catholic Church for the United States of America © 1994 United States Catholic Conference, Inc.—Libreria Editrice Vaticana. English translation of the Catechism of the Catholic Church: Modifications from the Editio Typica © 1997 United States Catholic Conference, Inc.—Libreria Editrice Vaticana. Compliant with The Roman Missal, Third Edition.

Printed in the United States of America. 21 20 19 18 17 / 5 4 3 2 1. Third Edition.

LIGUORI PUBLICATIONS
A Redemptorist Ministry

Final Activity

As you wrap up the lesson, ask the children to complete the "Living With Faith" activity on their own. Answers to the activity appear as follows.

1. Drying the dishes — A

2. Going to church — C

3. Searching online about a holy person — B

4. Calling a classmate who is sad — D or A

5. Going to your aunt's birthday party — D

6. Asking God for help before a test — C

7. Helping an injured player off the field — D

8. Reading a Bible story — B

9. Giving your allowance to the poor — A

10. Buying your friend a birthday gift — D

Closing Prayer

Say the Our Father together. Some children may not be familiar with this prayer yet, so you can also lead the Our Father as an echo prayer and have children repeat each line after you.

Take-Home

Ask the children to share today's lesson with their parents at home. Then ask the children to pick one way their family can grow in faith together this week.

Q3: Trinity: Three in One

Catechism: 232–67, 683–90

Objectives

- Define the Trinity as the name for the three persons in one God.
- Connect the Catholic teaching on the Trinity to God described in the Bible.
- Develop a relationship with each person of the Trinity.

Leader Meditation

Matthew 3:16–17

Think about your relationship with the Blessed Trinity. When you pray, do you tend to pray to God the Father, God the Son, or God the Holy Spirit? Spend time in prayer now for a deeper relationship with the person you seem to most overlook.

Leader Preparation

- Read the lesson, this lesson plan, the Scripture passage, and the *Catechism* sections. These sections will be helpful in responding to the questions of participants from all faith backgrounds or the children with no faith background.
- Be familiar with vocabulary terms for this lesson: Holy Trinity, person, God the Father, God the Son, God the Holy Spirit. Definitions are in this guide's glossary.
- Provide copies of a few prayers directed to each person of the Trinity. *Some suggestions include the Glory Be, the Sign of the Cross, Act of Consecration to the Blessed Trinity, In Praise of the Trinity from* The Roman Missal, *and St. Augustine's Prayer for Zeal.*

Welcome

As the children arrive, welcome any new inquirers and sponsors. Check for supplies and immediate needs. Ask for questions or comments about the last lesson that may have come up since then. Begin promptly.

Opening Scripture

Matthew 3:16–17

Light the candle and read aloud. Then, ask the children to point out where they see God the Father, God the Son, and God the Holy Spirit in this Scripture passage.

Jesus is God the Son. God the Father is the voice that comes from heaven. God the Holy Spirit is the dove, or Spirit of God, who descends from heaven.

The mystery of the Most Holy Trinity is the central mystery of Christian faith and life. It is the mystery of God in himself. It is therefore the source of all the other mysteries of faith, the light that enlightens them.

CCC 234

Trinity: Three in One

"I still don't get it," Terrence said, shaking his head. "Me and my dad are part of the same family. But we're not the same person. So how can Jesus and God both be the same? Jesus is the Son and God's the Father. Right?"

Mrs. Evans nodded and said, "It is confusing. That's why it's called a mystery of faith. Let's check Scripture and the *Catechism* for clues that might help us understand."

CCC 232–67, 683–90

Trinity: Three in One

After you read the anecdote for this section, discuss the reflection question as a group. If the children struggle to see how we can believe in three persons in one God, remind them about your lesson in faith from the previous session.

Revealing the Trinity

Give the children time to complete the chart on their own or with a partner. Walk around the room and help where needed. Affirm correct answers and gently guide the children back on track if they get distracted.

Suggested responses to the activity include:

- **God the Father** revealed himself in the Old Testament and God the Father taught the people of Israel about the one true God.

- **God the Son** became a man named Jesus. Jesus was both God and human. Jesus led a group of people called the apostles. He taught them about God, heaven, and how to live like him.

- **God the Holy Spirit** came to earth on a day we call Pentecost.

? *How do you think there can be just one God when we believe in God the Father, Son, and Holy Spirit?*

God's Name

"Christians are baptized in the name of the Father and of the Son and of the Holy Spirit: not in their names."

CCC 233

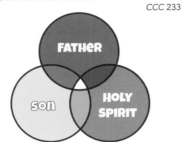

When you make and pray the Sign of the Cross, you say "in the *name* of the Father, the Son, and the Holy Spirit." We can address our prayers to God the Father, God the Son, or God the Holy Spirit. Each is a distinct person in one God. However, whether you pray to God the Father, God the Son, or God the Holy Spirit you are still praying to the same, one God.

It can be difficult to understand how there are three persons in one God, which is why it is sometimes called a mystery of faith. We call this mystery the **Holy Trinity** because *trinity* means "three" and God is holy. No one knew about this mystery until Jesus shared it with us. Through Jesus, God reveals himself as a union of three **persons**, "an eternal exchange of love, Father, Son, and Holy Spirit" (*CCC* 221).

Revealing the Trinity

God has been a trinity of persons forever! But we only learned about the Father, Son, and Spirit bit by bit, one at a time. God revealed this secret in three steps:

1. **God the Father** revealed himself to Abraham, Moses, David, and all the people of ancient Israel in the Old Testament. At the time, they worshiped many gods, but none of these gods was real. So God taught them that there is only one true God.

2. Much later, Jesus, **God the Son**, became a man. He had a group of friends he named the apostles. The apostles learned from Jesus that he was more than just another man. He was divine. Not only that, but Jesus was God! Jesus told them, "The Father and I are one" (John 10:30).

All three persons of the Trinity are revealed at Jesus' baptism. When Jesus is baptized, the voice of the Father says, "This is my beloved Son" (Matthew 3:17), and the Holy Spirit is seen descending upon Jesus like a dove.

3. **God the Holy Spirit** came down upon the Church at Pentecost. Mary, Jesus' mother, and his friends, the apostles, were praying together. The Holy Spirit came onto them and looked like flames of fire. This was the third step in revealing the Trinity. God is an eternal union of Father, Son, and Spirit.

God taught us about the Trinity bit by bit throughout history. God also helps us to know the Trinity better bit by bit in our own lives.

ACTIVITY

List one or two things you've learned about each person of the Trinity next to that person's name.

God the Father	
Jesus, God the Son	
God the Holy Spirit	

Symbols of the Trinity

It takes a long time to understand the mysteries of faith. Fortunately for us, some saints came up with examples to help us understand. Saint Patrick was a missionary to the Irish. He used a three-leaf clover to teach people about the Trinity. It's one clover with three leaves. It's both one *and* three.

Pope St. John Paul II used the example of a family. A family is one, but it's made up of several people: a mother, a father, and children. Like a human family, the Trinity is three persons united in love.

? How does your family teach you about God and God's love?

Responding to Love

"By the grace of Baptism…we are called to share in the life of the blessed Trinity" (*CCC* 265). Catholics are closest to the life of the Blessed Trinity when we celebrate the Eucharist at Mass. We also grow closer to the Trinity through prayer. You can pray to the Trinity just like you're talking to a friend.

Symbols of the Trinity

Ask the children to share the ways their family shares God's love.

Final Activity

As you wrap up the lesson, give children time to complete the "How Are They Similar?" activity. Answers to the activity are provided below.

- Pitcher, outfielder, shortstop
  All are part of a baseball team

- Teacher, principal, student
  All are part of a school

- King, queen, prince
  All are royalty or
  part of a royal family

- Toes, ankle, heel
  All are body parts,
  parts of the foot

- Sun, moon, stars
  All are objects in space

- Father, Son, Holy Spirit
  All are God

HOW ARE THEY SIMILAR?

What does each group below have in common?

✱ Pitcher, outfielder, shortstop _____

✱ Teacher, principal, student _____

✱ King, queen, prince _____

✱ Toes, ankle, heel _____

✱ Sun, moon, stars _____

✱ Father, Son, Spirit _____

In Short

- The Trinity is the term Christians use to signify the three persons in one God.
- The Trinity is revealed in Scripture.
- You can have a friendship with each person of the Trinity.

Journey of Faith for Children, Inquiry, Q3 (826351)
Imprimi Potest: Stephen T. Rehrauer, CSsR, Provincial, Denver Province, the Redemptorists.
Imprimatur: "In accordance with CIC 827, permission to publish has been granted on May 3, 2017, by Bishop Mark S. Rivituso, Vicar General, Archdiocese of St. Louis. Permission to publish is an indication that nothing contrary to Church teaching is contained in this work. It does not imply any endorsement of the opinions expressed in the publication, nor is any liability assumed by this permission."
Journey of Faith © 2000, 2017 Liguori Publications, Liguori, MO 63057. To order, visit Liguori.org or call 800-325-9521. Liguori Publications, a nonprofit corporation, is an apostolate of the Redemptorists. To learn more about the Redemptorists, visit Redemptorists.com. All rights reserved. No part of this publication may be reproduced, distributed, stored, transmitted, or posted in any form by any means without prior written permission.
Editors of the 2017 *Journey of Faith for Children:* Theresa Nienaber-Penuski and Pat Fosarelli, MD, DMin.
Design and production: Wendy Barnes, Lorena Mitre Jimenez, John Krus, and Bill Townsend. Illustrations: Jeff Albrecht.
Unless noted, Scripture texts in this work are taken from the *New American Bible,* revised edition © 2000, 1991, 1986, 1970 Confraternity of Christian Doctrine, Washington, D.C., and are used by permission of the copyright owner. All Rights Reserved. No part of the *New American Bible* may be reproduced in any form without permission in writing from the copyright owner. Excerpts from the English translation of the *Catechism of the Catholic Church for the United States of America* © 1994 United States Catholic Conference, Inc.—*Libreria Editrice Vaticana.* English translation of the *Catechism of the Catholic Church: Modifications from the Editio Typica* © 1997 United States Catholic Conference, Inc.—*Libreria Editrice Vaticana.* Compliant with *The Roman Missal, Third Edition.*
Printed in the United States of America. 21 20 19 18 17 / 5 4 3 2 1. Third Edition.

Closing Prayer

End with the *Glory Be*. The children may not be familiar with this prayer yet, so you may want to lead this as an echo prayer, display the words on the board, or have a handout for each child.

Glory be to the Father,
and to the Son,
and to the Holy Spirit;
as it was in the beginning,
is now, and ever shall be,
world without end. Amen.

Take-Home

Ask the children to continue researching the Trinity this week and find out one new thing about the Trinity to share at home. This can be a verse from Scripture, a prayer, something from the *Catechism*, or something from the life of a saint.

Q4: Who Is Jesus Christ?

Catechism: 514–682

Objectives

- Define Jesus as fully human and fully divine.
- Discover that Christ is the way to the Father and salvation.
- Develop participants' relationship with Jesus through personal sharing and reflection.

Leader Meditation

John 10:7–18

Jesus likens himself to a caring shepherd who would lay down his life for his sheep. Reflect on what these words tell us about the person Jesus.

Leader Preparation

- Read the lesson, this lesson plan, the Scripture passage, and the *Catechism* sections.
- Be familiar with the vocabulary terms for this lesson: Gospel, miracle. Definitions are given in the lesson and in this guide's glossary.
- Be prepared to model and review the steps to looking up Bible verses. There are many in this lesson. Determine ahead of time whether you can cover them all as a group, will divide them up for groups, or will leave some for participants to reflect on outside of the session.
- Ask your pastor for guidance on possible questions or concerns surrounding Jesus' life, identity, words, and dual natures. Perhaps he can help to lead the session or recommend ways to explain the material to the children.

Welcome

As the children arrive, welcome any new inquirers and sponsors. Check for supplies and immediate needs. Ask for any questions or comments about the last lesson that may have come up since then. Begin promptly.

Opening Scripture

John 10:7–18

Light the candle and read aloud. Emphasize the importance of Jesus' words, "I am the good shepherd. I know my own and my own know me." Clarify for the children what it means to be Jesus' own. As Jesus' own, we belong to Jesus' "flock" or family, just like we belong to our families. That doesn't mean Jesus "owns" us, like we are his slaves. You will discuss free will and making good choices in later lessons, so now may be a good time to focus on the idea that we belong to Jesus' "flock."

> As Lord, Christ is also head of the Church, which is his Body. Taken up to heaven and glorified after he had thus fully accomplished his mission, Christ dwells on earth in his Church.
>
> *CCC 669*

Who Is Jesus Christ?

Tomás was lost. He was supposed to be going to Terrence's house, but all the streets looked the same. Tomás knew he should probably turn around and go home, but he kept walking. Tomás knew he was way off track, but he didn't know how to get back on the right road.

"What are you doing way over here?" Terrence called when he saw Tomás.

Tomás felt relieved. "I'm lost. I didn't know where to go."

"That's OK. I'm walking my dog. If you walk back with us I can show you the way."

CCC: 514–682

Who Is Jesus Christ?

Read the lesson anecdote as a class and ask the children if they can think of a difference between the kind of lost Tomás was and the kind of lost Jesus talks about.

Tomás was physically lost. He thought he was on the correct street, but he wasn't. Terrence had to show him the right way to go. Jesus talks about us being lost spiritually. This means we might be mixed up about what choices are right or good, how to treat people, or how to behave.

The Way

Ask the children how Jesus could be the way to God. Emphasize that Jesus is like our spiritual map. Through his life, he gives us directions on how to get to God.

Ask the children to think about how Jesus leads them to God. Encourage them to think of specific stories and share a story of your own as an example.

The Truth

As a group, make a list of ways we know Jesus is the truth.

Jesus never lies. Jesus always does the things he says he'll do. Jesus cares about us and wants the best for us. When we do what Jesus says, we grow closer to God. Jesus is really God and wants us to go to heaven and be with him.

The Life

Pause here to do the "Jesus Is…" activity as a group. Emphasize that we know Jesus is God through his words and his actions.

• How does light help you see? How is Jesus like a light (John 8:12)?

Light clears away shadows and the dark so we can find our way and see the things around us. Jesus lights up our lives by helping us to tell right from wrong and to see the people around us.

• What does a shepherd do? How is Jesus like a shepherd (John 10:14)?

A shepherd takes care of sheep and keeps them safe and healthy. Jesus takes care of us and helps keep us safe by giving us rules to follow and showing us how to live. Jesus watches over us and listens to us when we talk to him.

Who Is Jesus?

Jesus is the most important person in our journey toward God. Jesus Christ is the center of our faith. Without Jesus, we couldn't know God. Without Jesus, there would be no Church.

Jesus said, "I am the way and the truth and the life. No one comes to the Father except through me" (John 14:6). Let's look at those words carefully.

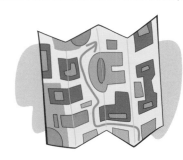

The Way

Jesus is the Way to God. When we know Jesus, we know God. What we learn from Jesus leads us closer to God.

How does Jesus lead you to God?

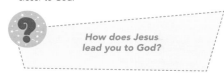

The Truth

Jesus didn't say, "What I *tell* you is the truth," but "I *am* the truth." Jesus asks us to believe in him because he is God. When we believe in someone, we trust what they say is true, too. That's why we also believe what Jesus taught.

Do you believe that Jesus is really God?

The Life

Jesus taught us how to live by his example. Jesus would often go off alone and pray. This helped him understand and obey his Father. We also spend time in prayer and live by God's rules. Jesus brings us everlasting life. That good news fills our lives with joy and hope.

What in your life brings you joy or hope?

Jesus Is…

Jesus didn't only perform good deeds. He also said a lot of things about himself. Here are a few:

• *"I am the light of the world"* (John 8:12). How does light help you see? How is Jesus like a light?

• *"I am the good shepherd"* (John 10:14). What does a shepherd do? How is Jesus like a shepherd?

• *"I am the true vine, and my Father is the vine grower"* (John 15:1). How does a vine help the plant it's attached to? How is Jesus like a vine?

• *"I am the bread of life"* (John 6:48). How does food give you life? How is Jesus like food?

• How does a vine help the plant it's attached to? How is Jesus like a vine (John 15:1)?

A vine keeps a plant rooted to the ground, where it can get nourishment and survive storms. A plant without a vine would wither up or blow away in a bad storm. Jesus keeps us "rooted" to God, where we can get spiritual nourishment and grow strong in our faith.

• How does food give you life? How is Jesus like food (John 6:48)?

Food nourishes our bodies and helps us stay active and healthy. Jesus helps our souls to stay active and healthy. Jesus nourishes our bodies and souls in a special way through the Eucharist.

The Life of Jesus

We read about Jesus' life in the **Gospels** of Matthew, Mark, Luke, and John. Jesus' birth was a miracle. God sent an angel named Gabriel to ask a girl named Mary if she was willing to be Jesus' mother. She was engaged to a man named Joseph. Jesus was born in Bethlehem, and Mary and Joseph helped him to grow knowing and loving God.

Jesus did many good things. He taught people about God. He forgave people when they were sorry for the wrong things they'd done. He also healed people who were sick or injured. Some of the most exciting stories about Jesus describe the miracles he performed. A **miracle** is an event that doesn't have a scientific explanation. It seems impossible, but there's proof that it happened.

Not everyone liked what Jesus was doing or saying. So the religious leaders of the time plotted to have Jesus killed on a cross. Jesus knew what they were planning, but he let them plot anyway. Jesus died on a cross, but three days later, the greatest miracle of all happened. Jesus rose from the dead! He appeared to his friends so they would know he was alive. Anyone who believes in Jesus knows that he is real and lives forever.

ACTIVITY

THE MIRACLES OF JESUS

Jesus performed a lot of miracles when he was on earth. What do these miracles teach us about Jesus?

- Matthew 14:22–33
  "[Jesus] came toward them, walking on the sea" (v. 25).

- Matthew 8:5–13
  "I will come and cure him" (v. 7).

- John 11:17–44
  "[Jesus] cried out in a loud voice, 'Lazarus, come out!'" (v. 43).

The Life of Jesus

Remind the children that the four Gospels appear in the New Testament and that the Gospels were written to teach us about Jesus.

Ask the whole group if they have heard any stories about miracles. While their examples don't need to be Church-approved miracles, be sure they see the difference between a miracle that's really attributed to God and something

people say is a "miracle" because it's just unexpected (like, "it's a *miracle* you cleaned your room without being asked").

Complete "The Miracles of Jesus" activity as a group; answers appear to the right. Because this activity comes before the children have learned how to navigate the Bible, help them locate the passages and read them aloud. Reading from a children's Bible storybook may be preferable with younger children.

• Matthew 14:22–33

This miracle reveals Jesus' divine nature (that Jesus is God) and that because Jesus is God he can command nature.

• Matthew 8:5–13

This miracle reveals that Jesus would accept Gentiles (people who weren't Jewish) as his followers, too. It also reveals Jesus' ability to heal us.

• John 11:17–44

This miracle reveals that Jesus, as God, had authority over death, and could bring people back to life.

Final Activity

As you wrap up the lesson, give the children time to complete the final activity of the lesson, "You Know Me." Ask the children to share one fact they learned about Jesus with the rest of the group. Walk around and see what the children are writing. Affirm good answers and help clarify any confusion.

"YOU KNOW ME"

List five things you learned about Jesus today.

1. _____

2. _____

3. _____

4. _____

5. _____

In Short

- Jesus is fully human and fully divine.
- Christ is the way to the Father and salvation.
- Your friendship with Jesus grows through sharing and reflection.

Journey of Faith for Children, Inquiry, Q4 (826351)
Imprimi Potest: Stephen T. Rehrauer, CSsR, Provincial, Denver Province, the Redemptorists.
Imprimatur: "In accordance with CIC 827, permission to publish has been granted on May 3, 2017, by Bishop Mark S. Rivituso, Vicar General, Archdiocese of St. Louis. Permission to publish is an indication that nothing contrary to Church teaching is contained in this work. It does not imply any endorsement of the opinions expressed in the publication, nor is any liability assumed by this permission."
Journey of Faith © 2000, 2017 Liguori Publications, Liguori, MO 63057. To order, visit Liguori.org or call 800-325-9521. Liguori Publications, a nonprofit corporation, is an apostolate of the Redemptorists. To learn more about the Redemptorists, visit Redemptorists.com. All rights reserved. No part of this publication may be reproduced, distributed, stored, transmitted, or posted in any form by any means without prior written permission.
Contributing writer: Francine M. O'Connor. Editors of the 2017 *Journey of Faith for Children:* Theresa Nienaber-Panuski and Pat Fosarelli, MD, DMin.
Design and production: Wendy Barnes, Lorena Mitre Jimenez, John Krus, and Bill Townsend. Illustrations: Jeff Albrecht.
Unless noted, Scripture texts in this work are taken from the *New American Bible,* revised edition © 2000, 1991, 1986, 1970 Confraternity of Christian Doctrine, Washington, D.C., and are used by permission of the copyright owner. All Rights Reserved. No part of the *New American Bible* may be reproduced in any form without permission in writing from the copyright owner. Excerpts from the English translation of the *Catechism of the Catholic Church for the United States of America* © 1994 United States Catholic Conference, Inc.—Libreria Editrice Vaticana. English translation of the *Catechism of the Catholic Church: Modifications from the Editio Typica* © 1997 United States Catholic Conference, Inc.—Libreria Editrice Vaticana. Compliant with *The Roman Missal, Third Edition.*
Printed in the United States of America. 21 20 19 18 17 / 5 4 3 2 1. Third Edition.

Liguori
PUBLICATIONS
A Redemptorist Ministry

Closing Prayer

Teach the children to pray the memorial acclamation below by asking them to repeat each line after you. Explain that these statements summarize our faith and declare who Jesus is. These lines are so important, we say them together at every Mass.

When we eat this Bread and drink this Cup, we proclaim your Death, O Lord, until you come again.

Take-Home

Ask the children and their parents or guardians to read John 1:1–18 together. Suggest splitting up the reading into one or two verses every night, depending on when your next session will be, so families have an opportunity to reflect together. Ask the children to please focus on how the passages talk about Jesus.

Q5: The Bible

Catechism: 74–83, 101–33, 109–19

Objectives

- Describe the Bible as both unique and historical.
- Define Scripture as the sacred and inspired word of God.
- Recognize that Scripture must be read carefully and thoughtfully.

Leader Meditation

2 Timothy 3:16–17

Reflect on these questions, then pray the prayer below. Do I take sufficient time each week to read and reflect on Scripture? When and how has God guided me through this sacred text, led me, and helped me make decisions about my life?

Dear God, you have given me the task of helping these young people understand your word. At times, I still struggle to understand it fully myself. Please send your Spirit to inspire and speak through me now, that I may become a bridge that connects your heart to the hearts and minds of my participants. Amen.

Leader Preparation

- Read the lesson, this lesson plan, the Scripture passage, and the *Catechism* sections.
- Be familiar with the vocabulary terms for this lesson: Bible, inspired, Old Testament, New Testament, Pentateuch, Torah, epistles. Definitions can be found in this guide's glossary.
- Make sure each participant has a Catholic Bible for the lesson and at home. Also gather materials and resources that assist them in studying and reflecting on Scripture and the Mass readings. If you can't provide physical Bibles for participants, give them a list of trusted Catholic translations and whether or not they can be found online.

Welcome

Greet the children as they arrive. Check for supplies and immediate needs. Solicit questions or comments about the previous lesson and/or share new information and findings. Begin promptly.

Opening Scripture

2 Timothy 3:16–17

Light the candle and read aloud. Ask each child to look up the passage and follow along in her or his own Bible rather than just listening to you read.

> Sacred Scripture is the speech of God as it is put down in writing under the breath of the Holy Spirit....[It] must be read and interpreted in the light of the same Spirit by whom it was written.
>
> Dogmatic Constitution on Divine Revelation (*Dei Verbum*), 9, 12; see *CCC* 81, 111

The Bible

"I get that Jesus was a real person. But how do you know he actually did all those things people said he did in the Bible? Isn't the Bible just a bunch of stories?" Lisa asked.

"The Bible isn't like a history textbook," Mrs. Evans answered. "We can't flip through it to pick out certain historical facts. But it's not a storybook, either. Everything the Bible teaches us about God and about how to live our lives is truth." Mrs. Evans held up her Bible, saying, "This is one of the most important things you can take with you on your faith journey."

CCC 74–83, 101–33, 109–19

The Bible

After you read the opening story, give the children time to complete the list activity. Not everything they've heard about the Bible will be aligned with Catholic teaching on the Bible. They may have heard others say, incorrectly, that "everything in the Bible has to be taken literally and exactly." That's OK for now. This list will just give you an idea of what the children have heard before today's lesson.

Who Wrote the Bible?

As a group, create a definition for the word *inspired* that applies to the authors of sacred Scripture.

The children may ask questions about the reliability of Scripture. If they do, point out that there is evidence both within Scripture itself and outside of it that roots them to historical events and eyewitness accounts. Encourage curious children to continue exploring Catholic resources on the history of the Bible. *CCC* "Article 3: Sacred Scripture" is a good place to start.

List two or three things you know or have heard about the Bible.

_____

_____

_____

What do you think it means to be inspired?

What Is the Bible?

The **Bible** is a collection of books about God and God's people. It begins when God created the world and all living things. The Bible tells about history and travels, victory and failure. There are stories, songs, blessings, and rules. It tells us how Jesus came into our world and how God wants us to live our faith.

Who Wrote the Bible?

It took hundreds of years and a lot of people to write the Bible we use today. But that doesn't mean the Bible is made up. The Bible is like a collection of memories people had about God, and through the inspiration of the Holy Spirit they were able to share those memories with the people who would come after them.

Because all those memories came from God, and because God is Truth, we know we can trust the truths in the Bible. The Holy Spirit **inspired** the biblical authors to write down their experiences and wisdom so everyone could hear God's word.

What's in the Bible?

There are different types of writing in the Bible: historical stories, poems, songs, and messages from God's prophets. We can't read a book of poems like a history book because they each have a different purpose. Poems use images to teach us about life or the world. History books give us facts about people, dates, and events. When we understand the kind of writing we're reading, we understand the Bible better.

The Bible has two main sections: the Old Testament and the New Testament. The **Old Testament** is about God's people before Jesus. It tells us about God's laws, how God helped his Chosen People, and even about the coming Messiah, Jesus. The **New Testament** tells us about Jesus and the things he taught when he was on earth. It also tells us about the early Church.

The Old Testament

The Old Testament took almost a thousand years to write. The first five books are called the **Pentateuch** or the **Torah**. These books explain the promises and laws between God and his people, the Israelites. God told his people he would send them a Messiah, a Savior. But the people didn't know who Jesus was. They waited, wondered, and prepared.

The New Testament

The New Testament starts when Jesus was born. The four Gospels teach us about Jesus' life on earth. Each Gospel is a little different because different people wrote each one. Each Gospel writer wanted to share a unique picture of Jesus so we could learn more about him. When we read the Gospels we hear, in Jesus' own words, what God and heaven are like. We read about Jesus' suffering, death, and resurrection. We learn how to live like Jesus.

Later, some disciples wrote letters to help build the first Church. These letters are called **epistles**. The first Christians loved Jesus so much they were willing to die for their faith.

How Do I Know What God Is Saying?

Sometimes the Bible might not make sense to you. Or it might seem like it doesn't have anything to do with your life. This makes it hard to believe God is speaking to you. When you read the Bible, please remember three things:

1. **God loves you** and wants to talk to you. Every story in the Bible is like a message from your best friend. God has something special and important to say just to you.

2. **Everyone needs help** reading the Bible. Listen to the people God sends to teach you, and ask all the questions you have.

3. **Prayer can open your mind and heart** to new ideas. If you're confused and no one is there to help you, just pray, "God, help me understand."

LOOKING UP VERSES

Tanya raised her hand. "So we have to read the whole Old Testament before we can learn about Jesus?"

Mrs. Evans shook her head. "No. The Bible isn't like a regular book. You don't have to read it from the beginning to the end. That's why when we talk about Bible passages we say, for example, Matthew 15:10. It's like a code.

"First comes the title of the book. Then the chapter number, then a colon, and finally the verse number. Most books have numbered chapters. When you look in that chapter for the verses, you'll find tiny numbers inside the paragraphs. When you find one that matches the verse number, that's what you read. We can look up Bible passages for anything. To learn when we have a question. For help when we're scared. Or even to pray."

Looking Up Verses

Pause to read the story in the lesson sidebar. Then ask the children to look up Matthew 15:10 on their own or with a partner, depending on how many Bibles you have to share. Check to make sure each child has found the correct passage.

If the children are struggling, pick more Bible verses to look up so the children become familiar with how to do it. Pick some of your favorite Scripture passages and share with the children why you like them so much. It's a great opportunity for the children to get to know you better as they learn. You can also use the Scripture passages from the "Final Activity."

As the children work, this is an opportunity to share more information on the Bible and how it is structured. You may want to share these points on the Old Testament:

- The books of the Old Testament are grouped to help us understand the journey of God's Chosen People.

- Each book has a particular purpose and was written in a unique style.

- There are forty-six books in the Old Testament of the *New American Bible,* revised edition, also called the *NABRE.*

And these points on the New Testament:

- There were several years of oral tradition before the early Christians felt the need to preserve their words in writing.

- By the end of the first century after Christ, nearly all of the twenty-seven books of the New Testament were written.

- Each book tells us something special about the person Jesus.

- Each book records the words and deeds of Jesus, and these records have the power to change how we live our lives today.

Final Activity

As you wrap up this lesson, give the children time to complete the "Exploring the Gospels" activity. You may not have enough time for the children to do all five questions, so you can divide the children into five groups and make each group responsible for one of the passages. Or assign the children a number from one to five and ask them to work independently on that passage.

If you cannot complete all five passages in class, encourage the children to complete them at home with their parents or another family member.

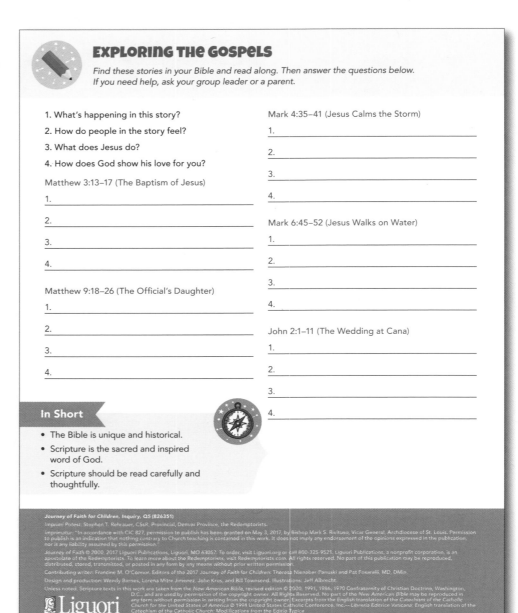

EXPLORING THE GOSPELS

Find these stories in your Bible and read along. Then answer the questions below. If you need help, ask your group leader or a parent.

1. What's happening in this story?
2. How do people in the story feel?
3. What does Jesus do?
4. How does God show his love for you?

Matthew 3:13–17 (The Baptism of Jesus)
1. _____
2. _____
3. _____
4. _____

Matthew 9:18–26 (The Official's Daughter)
1. _____
2. _____
3. _____
4. _____

Mark 4:35–41 (Jesus Calms the Storm)
1. _____
2. _____
3. _____
4. _____

Mark 6:45–52 (Jesus Walks on Water)
1. _____
2. _____
3. _____
4. _____

John 2:1–11 (The Wedding at Cana)
1. _____
2. _____
3. _____
4. _____

In Short

- The Bible is unique and historical.
- Scripture is the sacred and inspired word of God.
- Scripture should be read carefully and thoughtfully.

Journey of Faith for Children, Inquiry, Q5 (826351)

Imprimi Potest: Stephen T. Rehrauer, CSsR, Provincial, Denver Province, the Redemptorists.

Imprimatur: "In accordance with CIC 827, permission to publish has been granted on May 3, 2017, by Bishop Mark S. Rivituso, Vicar General, Archdiocese of St. Louis. Permission to publish is an indication that nothing contrary to Church teaching is contained in this work. It does not imply any endorsement of the opinions expressed in the publication, nor any liability assumed by this permission."

Journey of Faith © 2000, 2017 Liguori Publications, Liguori, MO 63057. To order, visit Liguori.org or call 800-325-9521. Liguori Publications, a nonprofit corporation, is an apostolate of the Redemptorists. To learn more about the Redemptorists, visit Redemptorists.com. All rights reserved. No part of this publication may be reproduced, distributed, stored, transmitted, or posted in any form by any means without prior written permission.

Contributing writer: Francine M. O'Connor. Editors of the 2017 *Journey of Faith for Children:* Theresa Nienaber Panuski and Pat Fosarelli, MD, DMin.

Design and production: Wendy Barnes, Lorena Mitre Jimenez, John Krus, and Bill Townsend. Illustrations: Jeff Albrecht.

Unless noted, Scripture texts in this work are taken from the *New American Bible*, revised edition © 2000, 1991, 1986, 1970 Confraternity of Christian Doctrine, Washington, D.C., and are used by permission of the copyright owner. All Rights Reserved. No part of the *New American Bible* may be reproduced in any form without permission in writing from the copyright owner. Excerpts from the English translation of the *Catechism of the Catholic Church* for the United States of America © 1994 United States Catholic Conference, Inc.—Libreria Editrice Vaticana. English translation of the *Catechism of the Catholic Church:* Modifications from the *Editio Typica* © 1997 United States Catholic Conference, Inc.—Libreria Editrice Vaticana. Compliant with *The Roman Missal, Third Edition.*

Printed in the United States of America. 21 20 19 18 17 / 5 4 3 2 1. Third Edition.

Liguori PUBLICATIONS
A Redemptorist Ministry

Suggested responses are below.

Matthew 3:13–17
The Baptism of Jesus

1. Jesus is baptized by John the Baptist and God the Father and God the Holy Spirit appear.

2. John the Baptist feels unworthy to baptize Jesus. God the Father and God the Spirit say they are pleased with Jesus.

3. Jesus gives John the authority to baptize him and God sends his Spirit down on Jesus.

4. Note: Participant responses will vary.

Matthew 9:18–26
The Official's Daughter

1. Jesus is healing the people. While he heals them physically, he tells them it is really their faith in him that has saved them.

2. The official is scared but fully trusts in Jesus' power.

3. Jesus heals the woman who touches his cloak and raises the official's daughter from the dead.

4. Note: Participant responses will vary.

Mark 4:35–41
Jesus Calms the Storm

1. The men on the boat are scared because there's a really bad storm outside. They wake up Jesus and he calms the storm.

2. They are panicking. They don't think they will survive the storm.

3. Jesus stays calm, and through his power he calms the storm.

4. Note: Participant responses will vary.

Mark 6:45–52
Jesus Walks on Water

1. Jesus walks on water back to the boat where his disciples are.

2. They are amazed, but some of their hearts are hardened (v. 52).

3. Jesus tells his disciples to have courage.

4. Note: Participant responses will vary.

John 2:1–11
The Wedding at Cana

1. Mary asks Jesus to provide more wine for the wedding celebration.

2. While not everyone knows where the wine came from, everyone believes it is the best wine.

3. Jesus listens to his mother and performs a miracle by turning water into wine.

4. Note: Participant responses will vary.

Closing Prayer

Read Hebrews 4:12 aloud, then explain to the group that reading Scripture can also be a kind of prayer. Conclude with this prayer:

God, may your words stay with me,
in my mind,
on my lips,
and in my heart.

May your words of love
never leave me.

You write every joy,
and every sadness
your word makes better.

Amen.

Take-Home

Ask the children to read a favorite Bible story out loud with their family this week. It can be from a children's Bible storybook or from the family Bible.

Q6: Where We Find God

Catechism: 27–100

Objectives

- Define revelation as the way God teaches us about himself and salvation.
- Discover that being human teaches us about God.
- List some of the many ways God shows himself to us.

Leader Meditation

John 16:13–15

Pray that you will grow in your openness to all God has revealed and his plan for your life.

Leader Preparation

- Read the lesson, this lesson plan, the Scripture passage, and the *Catechism* sections. Be prepared to answer questions about Church authority as it relates to sacred tradition.
- Magnifying glasses (if you can go outside) or slides of living things one might find in nature.
- Have art supplies for the children to use during the final activity.
- Be familiar with the vocabulary term for this lesson: divine revelation. The definition is provided in this guide's glossary.

Welcome

Greet the children as they arrive. Check for supplies and immediate needs. Solicit questions or comments about the previous lesson and/or share new information and findings. Begin promptly.

Opening Scripture

John 16:13–15

Light the candle and read aloud. After you've finished reading, ask the children what Jesus tells us in this passage.

The Spirit of truth will guide us to truth. The Spirit glorifies Jesus. Jesus has everything the Father has (because they are two persons in the same God). Through Jesus, God "declares" (gives) us everything that is his.

> The People of God as a whole never cease to welcome, to penetrate more deeply, and to live more fully from the gift of divine Revelation.
>
> *CCC 99*

Where We Find God

Tomás knew Terrence was around somewhere. He looked around very carefully. He couldn't see Terrence, and he couldn't hear Terrence, but Tomás knew he had to be here somewhere.

Then he saw it. Terrence's bright red-and-blue shoes! They revealed where Terrence was hiding. "I found you!" Tomás yelled.

CCC 27–100

Where We Find God

If you're able to go outside, give each child a magnifying glass and lead the children outside. They should also take their notebooks or prayer journal. Ask the children to spend time outside looking at nature up close and instruct them to choose three things to write about or draw in their journal.

As a group, ask each child to share one of those things and talk about how we can see God revealed in that thing.

For example, we can see God at work in a ladybug because each bug has a different number of spots. These spots show how God has made all living things unique and how everything God creates has a purpose. A ladybug's spots and bright coloring protect it from predators.

If you're unable to go outside, you can complete this activity by using pictures in a slide show or by asking the children to go around your classroom to find things that reveal God to us.

For example, if your classroom has a library you can point out how we learn about God in books, about the lives of the saints, or even from fiction books that teach us things like how to stand up for what is right or courageously fight evil.

We Can Find God

As you discuss conscience, ask the children if they've ever heard or seen a cartoon of a person trying to make a decision with a little angel on one shoulder and a devil on the other. While we don't literally have a little angel and devil telling us what to do, our conscience is kind of like that. In our hearts, we know what's right (the angel), but sometimes sin (the devil) tries to lead us away from what's right.

Talk about the first discussion question on the next page of the participant lesson as a group: "Why should we listen to our conscience?" List the reasons on the board or ask the children to take notes.

Give the children some quiet time to reflect on the other two discussion questions on their own. Tell them to mark this page so they can come back to it. These questions and the children's responses will be a good starting place for an examination of conscience as children prepare to receive the sacrament of reconciliation.

We Can Find God

Even if we can't see God as a person, he still shows himself to us. When God shows himself, it's called **divine revelation**. Saint Paul tells us that God "wills everyone to be saved and to come to knowledge of the truth" (1 Timothy 2:4). That means God wants us to know him and hear his word. The catechism says that "the desire for God is written in the human heart" (*CCC* 27).

This means God created us to want to find God! God gave us this desire so that we would want to find him in the world. Our desire for God helps us when we look for him because it sends us in the right direction. It's kind of like:

- a person in the dark turning on a flashlight to see where to go;
- a flower growing toward the sun;
- a ship in a storm heading for the lighthouse.

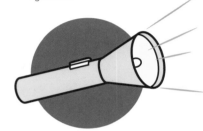

ACTIVITY
WHERE'S GOD HIDING?

Let's be detectives. See where you can find clues of where God is hidden in creation.

Spend some time outside or with your group leader and collect evidence of where God's hiding. Is God hiding in a flower? A bug? A tree? Write down or draw pictures of all the places you think God might be hiding in nature.

If you can't go outside, find clues of where God's hiding inside. Is he hiding in a book? A picture? Your teacher? Write down or draw pictures of all the places you think God might be hiding inside.

God also gave us an inner voice, called our conscience, so we can know right from wrong and then choose what's good. We use our consciences when we:

- want to be kind and do what's right.
- know what to do (or *not* to do) without being told.
- see goodness in God's creations (people and things!).
- trust others.

Why should we listen to our conscience?

Have you ever ignored your conscience and done something you knew was wrong?

Did that make you feel good or bad? Why?

Knowing God

We learn about God piece by piece. Right now, our picture of God is like a puzzle. The empty spaces are pieces about God we haven't learned yet. It's not always easy to know where a piece goes in a puzzle without seeing the whole picture first. That's why God helps us by showing himself to us.

God reveals himself to us in three special ways:

1. **Sacred Scripture:** God inspired the words in the Bible. The Holy Spirit helped the authors write it. When we read the Bible, we see God better.

2. **Sacred Tradition:** Inspired by the Holy Spirit, the apostles shared special practices and teachings with the members of the early Church. These traditions helped people understand Jesus' words and actions better. We still follow these traditions in the Church today. When we follow sacred Tradition, we learn more about God.

3. **The magisterium:** This is the "teaching voice" of the Catholic Church. The pope and bishops have a special job: to teach God's people using the authority given to them by Jesus. Together these men make up the magisterium. It is the job of the magisterium to explain difficult things in ways we can understand so we can understand God better.

Sacred Tradition: When Jesus was on earth, he gave the Church special practices (like the sacraments and the Mass) we still carry out today. This connects us to our Church family because we all share these traditions and have shared them through generations. These are similar to the traditions we have with our families, like eating a certain food over the holidays, putting out special decorations, or playing a certain game. Even if we aren't around all of our family all the time, we can be connected by these traditions.

The magisterium: Religion can be complicated and not always easy for us to understand. That's why we have special teachers who help explain difficult things in a way that makes it easier for us to start learning about them. It's just like learning any difficult subject. We have to rely on teachers to help us understand, and we sometimes can't learn everything all at once. Just like solving a complex math problem, you have to start with counting, then adding and subtracting, and keep building from there.

Knowing God

As you discuss the three special ways God reveals himself to us, give an example (or ask the children for an example) of how we can learn about God this way and an example of how we can learn about someone else through a similar way. This will help the children connect that learning more about God is about building a relationship with God, not just acquiring knowledge.

Sacred Scripture: *In the New Testament, we learn about Jesus' life and the things he did while he was on earth. Through these accounts, we learn more about Jesus and what he was like so we can grow to be more like him. This is similar to reading stories about the lives of the saints or even letters from our relatives. The more we read about someone's life, the more we can get to know that person.*

Final Activity

Go over the verses from Psalm 139 and emphasize that God isn't some giant figure looming over everything we do. Rather, God is like our best friend who does everything by our side. Learning about God is like making a new friend, and when we make new friends, we like to do things together.

As the students draw, encourage them to choose an activity that tells God something about them, and then encourage them to keep God in mind the next time they do this activity.

 BEING CLOSE TO GOD

God loves you personally and brought you to life. How close is God to you, even when you don't know it? These verses from Psalm 139 give us an idea:

- "You know when I sit and stand" (verse 2).
- "Before a word is on my tongue, LORD, you know it all" (4).
- "You encircle me" (5).

- "You knit me in my mother's womb" (13).
- "My bones are not hidden from you" (15).
- "In your book...my days were shaped" (16).

God is with us all the time! In everything we do! What's your favorite thing to do? Draw a picture of you and God doing it together as friends.

In Short

- Revelation teaches us about God and salvation.
- Being human teaches us about God.
- God shows himself to us in many ways.

Journey of Faith for Children, Inquiry, Q6 (826351)

Imprimi Potest: Stephen T. Rehrauer, CSsR, Provincial, Denver Province, the Redemptorists.

Imprimatur: "In accordance with CIC 827, permission to publish has been granted on May 3, 2017, by Bishop Mark S. Rivituso, Vicar General, Archdiocese of St. Louis. Permission to publish is an indication that nothing contrary to Church teaching is contained in this work. It does not imply any endorsement of the opinions expressed in the publication, nor is any liability assumed by this permission."

Journey of Faith © 2000, 2017 Liguori Publications, Liguori, MO 63057. To order, visit Liguori.org or call 800-325-9521. Liguori Publications, a nonprofit corporation, is an apostolate of the Redemptorists. To learn more about the Redemptorists, visit Redemptorists.com. All rights reserved. No part of this publication may be reproduced, distributed, stored, transmitted, or posted in any form by any means without prior written permission.

Contributing writer: Deacon Stephen F. Miletic, PhD. Editors of the 2017 *Journey of Faith for Children:* Theresa Nienaber-Panuski and Pat Fosarelli, MD, DMin.

Design and production: Wendy Barnes, Lorena Mitre Jimenez, John Krus, and Bill Townsend. Illustrations: Jeff Albrecht.

Unless noted, Scripture texts in this work are taken from the *New American Bible,* revised edition © 2010, 1991, 1986, 1970 Confraternity of Christian Doctrine, Washington, D.C., and are used by permission of the copyright owner. All Rights Reserved. No part of the *New American Bible* may be reproduced in any form without permission in writing from the copyright owner. Excerpts from the English translation of the *Catechism of the Catholic Church for the United States of America* © 1994 United States Catholic Conference, Inc.—Libreria Editrice Vaticana. English translation of the *Catechism of the Catholic Church: Modifications from the Editio Typica* © 1997 United States Catholic Conference, Inc.—Libreria Editrice Vaticana. Compliant with *The Roman Missal, Third Edition.*

Printed in the United States of America. 21 20 19 18 17 / 5 4 3 2 1. Third Edition.

Liguori PUBLICATIONS
A Redemptorist Ministry

Closing Prayer

Read aloud this prayer of St. Augustine (*CCC* 30), asking children to listen closely:

You are great, O Lord, and greatly to be praised: great is your power and your wisdom is without measure. And man, so small a part of your creation, wants to praise you....You yourself encourage him to delight in your praise, for you have made us for yourself, and our heart is restless until it rests in you.

See Confessions, Book 1, Chapter 1

Take-Home

As the children begin to think about their relationship with God as a friendship, encourage them to "introduce" their new friend to their family this week. They can do this by sharing a favorite Bible story about Jesus, by praying before dinner (or any other family activity), and asking God to be present.

Q7: Your Prayer Life

Catechism: 2558–65; 2725–45

Objectives

- Describe prayer as talking with God.
- Identify and practice basic forms and styles of Christian prayer.
- Realize there are many ways to pray, such as individually and as a group, with formal prayers or spontaneous thoughts.

Leader Meditation

John 16:23–27 and Matthew 18:19–20

Jesus tells us something very important about the power of prayer in each of these passages. Which modes of prayer are most comfortable for you? How much time do you spend in prayer preparing for these lessons?

Leader Preparation

- Read the lesson, this lesson plan, the Scripture passages, and the *Catechism* sections.
- Bring art supplies for the participants to create their own prayer. If you're not doing this activity, find a space for class that will allow participants to spread out and reflect on the different prayer styles instead.

Welcome

Greet the children as they arrive. Check for supplies and immediate needs. Solicit questions or comments about the previous lesson and/or share new information and findings. Begin promptly.

Opening Scripture

John 16:23–27 and Matthew 18:19–20

Light the candle and read aloud. Before beginning your discussion of the lesson handout, ask the children what kinds of things they might pray about or if they have a favorite prayer.

"Pray constantly" (1 Thessalonians 5:17). It is always possible to pray. It is even a vital necessity. Prayer and Christian life are inseparable.

CCC 2757

Your Prayer Life

"Do you talk to God?" Tanya asked Tomás as they walked home from school.

"What do you mean?"

"Mrs. Evans is always saying we should be praying outside of class, but I don't know how to talk to God like that."

"I think you can talk to God however you want. I always pray with my grandma. Sometimes we just tell God about our days. Other times we pray the same prayers together. My grandma says the important thing is to make God part of your life."

CCC 2558–65, 2725–45

Your Prayer Life

After reading the story together, ask the children if they've ever been worried they're praying wrong or afraid to pray. If a lot of children raise their hands, ask them to state their fears, make a list on the board, and talk about each fear. After you've addressed each fear, cross it off the list and tell the children they no longer have to worry about it before they pray.

For example, if the children say they're afraid to pray because they aren't sure they're praying correctly, write "not praying correctly" on the board. Then tell the children that "as you'll learn in today's lesson there is no wrong way to pray as long as your goal is a conversation with God. Cross that fear off the list!"

Talking With God

As a group, create a list to answer the question, "How do you talk to God?" If your list is short or the children all say the same thing, broaden the question to, "What are some ways we can talk to God?" and encourage the children to be creative. You can even contribute some ideas of your own.

Give the children time to answer the two reflection questions at the end of this section on their own. You can invite volunteers to share their responses or share a time you didn't listen to God or listened to God even when it was hard.

Prayers Using Words

After you've gone through the list of prayer types, go around the room and ask each child to give an example of a time where we could offer a prayer of praise, apology, thanks, or hope. You can make this activity more difficult by not allowing the same prayer type to be used twice in a row.

Give the children time to complete the reflection questions activity at the end of this section. If you have time, divide the children into four groups and assign each group a bullet point. Ask the children in each group to share their list with the rest of the groups.

JOURNEY OF FAITH | INQUIRY

Talking With God

Prayer is talking with God. When we talk to someone, most of the time we use words. We ask for something. We say thank you. We share secrets. But we don't always use words to tell things to our closest friends. Have you ever just looked at your best friend and known what he or she was thinking? You didn't need words to say, "Can you believe that?" Or, "Wasn't that funny?"

 God knows you better than your closest friend. So you don't always need words to talk to God. We can talk with God by being in nature, visiting a holy place, or speaking with him in the Eucharist. We can talk to God by doing something nice for someone. We can talk to God by reading his word in the Bible or by drawing God a picture.

Sometimes we laugh with God. Sometimes we cry with God. Sometimes when we talk to God we're so happy we just want to sing and jump. Other times we're angry with God and just want to shout.

 How do you talk to God?

It's important we don't just talk to God. We have to listen, too. Just like we listen when our best friend has something to tell us. We have to listen very carefully when God talks to us. God speaks directly to our hearts, not our ears, and it's not always easy to hear God's voice.

Luckily, God knows it's sometimes hard for us to hear him. God knows we might not be good at waiting and listening. God knows we might get distracted. But God is very patient. Even if we don't do a good job of listening the first time, God will still talk to us when we are ready to sit still and be with him.

 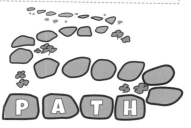 **Is it sometimes hard for you to listen?**

How can you be a good listener for God?

PATH

Prayers Using Words

There are lots of ways you can pray using your words. We can group these word prayers into four types. You can remember these types by thinking of the abbreviation "P.A.T.H."

Praise: God is so amazing that we want to let everyone know. A prayer of praise is one that says, "God, you're awesome!" Or, "God, I want to tell everyone how great you are!"

Apology: We all know what it's like to do something we wish we hadn't done. Or to do something we shouldn't have done. This is prayer that says, "God, I'm sorry."

Thanks: When we receive a gift, we thank the person who gave it to us. God gives us things, too. In fact, God gives us everything we have. This prayer says, "Thank you, God!"

Hope: We all hope for things to happen in our lives or for people we care about. This prayer asks God to help us with those things we hope for. We might say, "God, please help me pass this test," or, "God, please help my sick friend get better."

It's important for us to talk to God in all these different ways. It's easy to ask God for a lot of things, but we also have to say "thank you" and "I'm sorry," too.

ACTIVITY

What makes it hard to:

- praise God?

- tell God you're sorry?

- thank God?

- ask God for something?

When We Don't Get What We Pray for

Jesus said, "Ask and you will receive" (Luke 11:9). Sometimes people think that means God will get them exactly what they want as soon as they ask for it. That doesn't always happen. When you don't get what you pray for that doesn't mean God wasn't listening or that God doesn't care about you.

Your parents don't always give you what you want either. You might want cupcakes for dinner every night, but that wouldn't be healthy. Your dad would probably say no. But that doesn't mean he doesn't love you or that he ignored you.

God wants us to have what's best for us. Sometimes we think something is the best for us (like cupcakes), but it could actually hurt us or lead us away from God. Sometimes, we ask for something without thinking it through or because we don't want to do something the hard way:

- You ask for a dog, but you can't take care of one.

- You ask for an "A" on a test, but you didn't study for it.

- You ask for a new friend after you and your friend have a fight, but what you really need is to make up with your friend.

Sometimes, what we ask for is very serious and we don't understand why God won't give us what we pray for. Sometimes God's response to our prayer makes us very sad:

- You ask that your grandpa gets better, but he stays sick.

- You ask that your parents stop fighting, but they don't.

- You ask that your mom stay home, but she always has to go to work.

We don't know why God doesn't answer every prayer like we want him to, especially when our prayers seem like they would be good for everyone. When we have faith, we trust that God knows how to answer our prayers best—even when we're sad.

When We Don't Get What We Pray for

As you discuss this section, emphasize that God *does* always listen to us and answer our prayers. Sometimes that answer is "no" or "not yet."

If the children still struggle with this section, share an age-appropriate example from your own life of a time when hearing "no" turned out to be a good thing.

Final Activity

As you wrap up your lesson, give the children time to complete "In Your Own Words," the final activity. Have art supplies (crayons, markers, construction paper, stickers, and anything else you can think of) ready for the children to decorate their prayer.

Encourage them to use what they learned today in the words they use by making their prayer meaningful to them. Children can write a prayer of praise, apology, thanks, hope, or a combination of the four.

As the children create, walk around and offer help as needed. As you walk, ask the children what type of prayer they've chosen. As you circulate, clarify any points of confusion that come up.

 IN YOUR OWN WORDS

In the space below, write or draw your own prayer to God.

In Short

- Prayer is talking with God.
- Prayer can be personal or done with a group.
- Prayer can be done in a lot of ways.

Journey of Faith for Children, Inquiry, Q7 (826351)
Imprimi Potest: Stephen T. Rehrauer, CSsR, Provincial, Denver Province, the Redemptorists.
Imprimatur: "In accordance with CIC 827, permission to publish has been granted on May 3, 2017, by Bishop Mark S. Rivituso, Vicar General, Archdiocese of St. Louis. Permission to publish is an indication that nothing contrary to Church teaching is contained in this work. It does not imply any endorsement of the opinions expressed in the publication, nor is any liability assumed by this permission."
Journey of Faith © 2000, 2017 Liguori Publications, Liguori, MO 63057. To order, visit Liguori.org or call 800-325-9521. Liguori Publications, a nonprofit corporation, is an apostolate of the Redemptorists. To learn more about the Redemptorists, visit Redemptorists.com. All rights reserved. No part of this publication may be reproduced, distributed, stored, transmitted, or posted in any form by any means without prior written permission.
Editors of the 2017 Journey of Faith for Children: Theresa Nienaber-Panuski and Pat Fosarelli, MD, DMin.
Design and production: Wendy Barnes, Lorena Mitre Jimenez, John Krus, and Bill Townsend. Illustrations: Jeff Albrecht.
Unless noted, Scripture texts in this work are taken from the New American Bible, revised edition © 2010, 1991, 1986, 1970 Confraternity of Christian Doctrine, Washington, D.C., and are used by permission of the copyright owner. All Rights Reserved. No part of the New American Bible may be reproduced in any form without permission in writing from the copyright owner. Excerpts from the English translation of the Catechism of the Catholic Church for the United States of America © 1994 United States Catholic Conference, Inc.—Libreria Editrice Vaticana. English translation of the Catechism of the Catholic Church: Modifications from the Editio Typica © 1997 United States Catholic Conference, Inc.—Libreria Editrice Vaticana. Compliant with The Roman Missal, Third Edition.
Printed in the United States of America. 21 20 19 18 17 / 5 4 3 2 1. Third Edition.

Liguori
PUBLICATIONS
A Redemptorist Ministry

Closing Prayer

Pray spontaneously using one of the four prayer types discussed in this lesson. You might want to offer a prayer of hope for each child as they continue in their journey to the Church, or a prayer of thanks for everything you've learned today.

Take-Home

Ask the children to share what they've learned at home by leading a family dinner prayer sometime (or multiple times!) before your next meeting.

Q8: Catholic Prayers

Catechism: 524, 971, 1168–73, 2759–72

Objectives

- Recognize how personal and traditional prayers connect us to God in different ways.
- Realize that the mysteries of the rosary reflect the mysteries of Christ.
- Discover a few of the many traditional Catholic prayers and try them out.

Leader Meditation

Acts 2:42–47

Many people leave the Church and return later because they miss the tradition and the rituals that bond all Catholics to the ancient Church. If you couldn't attend Church, which traditions would you miss most? Which traditions bind you most closely to God? Which traditions bring you into closest contact with Jesus and his teachings? Meditate on what it means for you to be Catholic.

Leader Preparation

- Read the lesson, this lesson plan, the Scripture passage, and the *Catechism* sections.
- Consider asking your parish to donate rosaries or another prayer help for the children in your class and hand them out at an appropriate time during the lesson. Note: Handing them out as the children arrive may distract them from the lesson.
- If your parish typically uses different wording for the prayers than what appears in the children's handout, have a sheet with those versions for children to pick up.
- If you have any other sacramentals that mean something to you, bring them in to show your class and encourage sponsors to do the same. *Examples: prayer cards, breviary, rosary, monstrance, holy water, icon, statue, or a scapular.*
- Be familiar with the vocabulary terms for this lesson: hallowed, trespasses, womb, rosary. Definitions are provided in this guide's glossary.

Welcome

Greet the children as they arrive. Check for supplies and immediate needs. Solicit questions or comments about the previous lesson and/or share new information and findings. Begin promptly.

Opening Scripture

Acts 2:42–47

Light the candle and read aloud. As you begin your lesson, ask the children to keep in mind how the early Church used special prayers and group prayer as ways to stay united with each other and with Jesus.

> The tradition of Christian prayer is one of the ways in which the tradition of faith takes shape and grows, especially through the contemplation and study of believers.
>
> CCC 2651; see Dogmatic Constitution on Divine Revelation (*Dei Verbum*), 8

Catholic Prayers

After their last RCIA session on prayer, Mrs. Evans invited the children to come next time ready to share their favorite way to pray. Tomás was excited. He and his grandma shared a special prayer every week when he went to visit her. He couldn't wait to share it with his class.

"My favorite prayer is called the rosary," Tomás announced. "It's made up of a lot of different prayers, like the Our Father. The Our Father was Jesus' prayer from the Bible. And the Hail Mary."

"I've never heard of those prayers before," Tanya said. "Could you teach me?"

"Sure!" Tomás was happy he could share his favorite prayer.

CCC 524, 971, 1168–73, 2759–72

Catholic Prayers

After reading, ask for volunteers to share their response to the reflection question, "How do you and your family pray?"

Sign of the Cross

Model the Sign of the Cross for the children and then ask them to practice it on their own. You may also use this as a chance for extra practice—and to get out some extra energy—by asking the children to practice genuflecting while making the Sign of the Cross like they'll do when they enter church. You can also quiz them on where they should face when genuflecting in church: They should face the tabernacle, where Jesus is present, and not necessarily the front of church where the altar is.

Our Father

Start by reading the Our Father from Matthew 6:9–13 and discuss the meaning of the prayer with the children.

If your parish regularly uses alternate wording—like, "forgive us our sins" or "forgive us our debts" instead of "forgive us our trespasses"—practice that version with the children, too. If you have a special prayer sheet prepared for the children, pass that out now so the children can follow along.

Catholics love to pray together. It brings us together as a community. That's why Catholics have so many formal prayers. When we pray as a group, it's like we're having a conversation with God and the rest of our friends!

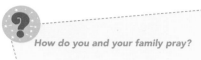

? *How do you and your family pray?*

Sign of the Cross

This prayer honors the Holy Trinity. We use this all the time, like during Mass and when we bless ourselves with holy water. We say: *In the name of the Father, and of the Son, and of the Holy Spirit* while touching our forehead, chest, and shoulders. Then we say: *Amen* and bring our hands together. Watch your teacher and then try it on your own!

In the name of the Father,   **and of the Son,**

and of the Holy...   **...Spirit**

Our Father

This prayer honors God the Father. Jesus taught his friends this prayer when they asked him how to pray (Matthew 6:9–14, Luke 11:1–4). We can pray it alone, with our families, and at Mass. Other Christians pray this prayer, too!

> *Our Father, who art in heaven,*
> *hallowed be thy name;*
> *thy kingdom come;*
> *thy will be done on earth as it is in heaven.*
> *Give us this day our daily bread;*
> *and forgive us our trespasses*
> *as we forgive those who trespass against us;*
> *and lead us not into temptation,*
> *but deliver us from evil. Amen*
> *(see Matthew 6:9–13).*

This prayer says that God is the Father and ruler of us all and that he lives in heaven. **Hallowed** means "holy." So we pray God's name will be used in a holy way. We want God's kingdom to come to us on earth, because his kingdom is full of peace and joy. We ask God for food and the other things we need. **Trespasses** is another word for "wrongs" or "sins." We ask God to forgive our sins. We also promise to forgive those who hurt us. Finally, we ask God to save us from evil and help us to choose good over bad.

Hail Mary

Hail Mary, full of grace,
the Lord is with you;
blessed are you among women,
and blessed is the fruit of your womb,
*   Jesus.*
Holy Mary, Mother of God,
pray for us sinners now
and at the hour of our death. Amen.

This prayer honors the Mother of Jesus, Mary. "Hail Mary, full of grace" are the words the angel Gabriel used when he told Mary she would give birth to Jesus. This prayer says, "Hello, Mary. You are full of God's loving Spirit! You are the greatest of all women."

A **womb** is where a baby grows before he or she is born, so a "fruit" of the womb is a baby. For Mary, that was Jesus. God the Father made Mary holy and without sin so she could become the Mother of God.

We also pray to and honor Mary through the **rosary**, a special prayer we pray using counted beads. The rosary includes many Hail Marys and other prayers.

The Glory Be

Glory be to the Father, and to the Son,
*   and to the Holy Spirit;*
as it was in the beginning, is now, and ever
*   shall be, world without end. Amen.*

This prayer honors the Trinity. As a sign of respect for God, many people bow at the waist when they say it.

Practice saying the Glory Be while bowing.

The Act of Contrition

Oh my God, I am sorry for my sins
with my whole heart. In choosing to do
wrong and failing to do good,
I have sinned against you and your Church.
I firmly intend, with your help,
to make up for my sins,
to sin no more,
and to love you as I should. Amen.

This special prayer tells God we are sorry for the bad things we have done. Our sins push us away from God. When we tell God we're sorry, we get closer to God. The same way when we hurt our friend we don't feel like friends any more, but when we say we're sorry we heal our friendship. We never want to hurt God or the people we care about. So we intend, or promise, to say we're sorry, try to fix any messes our sins caused, and to treat others and God better the next time.

i'm sorry

Hail Mary

If you have rosaries to share with the children, this is a good opportunity to pass them out. You can practice the Hail Mary by praying the first three beads. You can say the first one on your own, have the children repeat after you for the second, and pray altogether for the third.

You can also show the children which beads on the rosary they'd use to pray the Our Father, the Glory Be, and the Sign of the Cross.

Emphasize how each decade of the rosary focuses on a different part of Jesus' life. If you have time, list all the mysteries of the rosary for your group.

Final Activity

As you wrap up the lesson, give the children time to complete the final fill-in-the-blank activity. To add more to this activity, ask the children to pray the prayer silently after they've filled in all the blanks.

COMPLETE THE PRAYERS

Fill in the blanks using the word bank below. Some words will be used more than once.

now	earth	full	Holy Spirit	sinners	evil
heaven	bread	God	Jesus	temptation	Son
Father	beginning	forgive	blessed	kingdom	trespasses

Our Father, who art in _____,

hallowed be thy name;

thy _____ come;

thy will be done

on _____ as it is in _____.

Give us this day our daily _____;

and forgive us our _____

as we _____ those who trespass

    against us;

and lead us not into _____,

but deliver us from _____.

Amen.

Hail Mary, _____ of grace,

the Lord is with you;

_____ are you among women,

   of your womb, _____,

Holy Mary, Mother of _____,

pray for us _____

_____ and at the hour of our death.

Amen.

Glory be to the _____,

and to the _____,

and to the _____;

as it was in the _____,

is now,

and ever shall be,

world without end.

Amen.

In Short

- Personal and traditional prayers connect us to God in different ways.
- The mysteries of the rosary reflect the mystery of Christ.
- There are many traditional Catholic prayers.

Journey of Faith for Children, Inquiry, Q8 (826351)

Imprimi Potest: Stephen T. Rehrauer, CSsR, Provincial, Denver Province, the Redemptorists.

Imprimatur: "In accordance with CIC 827, permission to publish has been granted on May 3, 2017, by Bishop Mark S. Rivituso, Vicar General, Archdiocese of St. Louis. Permission to publish is an indication that nothing contrary to Church teaching is contained in this work. It does not imply any endorsement of the opinions expressed in the publication; nor is any liability assumed by this permission."

Journey of Faith © 2000, 2017 Liguori Publications, Liguori, MO 63057. To order, visit Liguori.org or call 800-325-9521. Liguori Publications, a nonprofit corporation, is an apostolate of the Redemptorists. To learn more about the Redemptorists, visit Redemptorists.com. All rights reserved. No part of this publication may be reproduced, distributed, stored, transmitted, or posted in any form by any means without prior written permission.

Editors of the 2017 *Journey of Faith for Children:* Theresa Nienaber-Panuski and Pat Fosarelli, MD, DMin.

Design and production: Wendy Barnes, Lorena Mitre Jimenez, John Krus, and Bill Townsend. Illustrations: Jeff Albrecht.

Unless noted, Scripture texts in this work are taken from the *New American Bible*, revised edition © 2000, 1991, 1986, 1970 Confraternity of Christian Doctrine, Washington, D.C., and are used by permission of the copyright owner. All Rights Reserved. No part of the *New American Bible* may be reproduced in any form without permission in writing from the copyright owner. Excerpts from the English translation of the *Catechism of the Catholic Church* for the United States of America © 1994 United States Catholic Conference, Inc.—Libreria Editrice Vaticana; English translation of the *Catechism of the Catholic Church:* Modifications from the *Editio Typica* © 1997 United States Catholic Conference, Inc.—Libreria Editrice Vaticana. Compliant with *The Roman Missal, Third Edition.*

Printed in the United States of America. 21 20 19 18 17 / 5 4 3 2 1 Third Edition.

Liguori PUBLICATIONS
A Redemptorist Ministry

Closing Prayer

Ask the children for any special intentions. Then close with a prayer from the lesson. Take a vote on which prayer from today was the group's favorite and pray that one. Or if you have some extra time, pray all the prayers from today or a decade of the rosary.

Take-Home

Ask the children to share their favorite prayer from today with their family. If their family is already familiar with these prayers, challenge them to lead or co-lead a whole rosary with their family.

Q9: The Mass

Catechism: 1341–1419

Objectives

- Distinguish between the two parts of the Mass.
- Identify most major actions and events during the Mass by their function and importance.
- Begin to recognize Jesus' Real Presence in the Eucharist.

Leader Meditation

Luke 22:14–20

Reflect on the meaning the Mass has for you. Make a renewed effort to remain focused and connected during Mass next Sunday. When you receive the Body and Blood of our Lord, try to do so with unwavering affirmation that you recognize you are receiving the Real Presence of Jesus Christ.

Leader Preparation

- Read the lesson, this lesson plan, the Scripture passage, and the *Catechism* sections.
- Be familiar with the vocabulary terms for this lesson: procession, *Gloria*, Liturgy of the Word, *Lectionary*, Responsorial Psalm, *Alleluia*, homily, Universal Prayer, petitions, Liturgy of the Eucharist, offertory, eucharistic prayer, "Holy, Holy, Holy." Definitions are in this guide's glossary. Additional information and details are available in *The Roman Missal*.
- If possible, make a copy of the petitions from the coming week's Sunday Mass to use as the closing prayer or create a list of petitions with the group as part of today's lesson.
- Gather Mass and Mass-reading resources: a copy of *The Roman Missal*, the *Lectionary*, etc.

Welcome

Greet the children as they arrive. Check for supplies and immediate needs. Solicit questions or comments about the previous lesson and/or share new information and findings. Begin promptly.

Opening Scripture

Luke 22:14–20

Light the candle and read aloud. Suggest that the children imagine they are gathered around a table with Jesus and are hearing these words from him. Ask them to picture Jesus sharing the bread and the wine with them personally. Before beginning your discussion of the handout, ask the children if this reading reminded them of anything.

If no one says, "Mass," or "the Eucharist," you may need to give the children hints to lead into it, like, "It's a meal Catholics share with each other every Sunday."

It was above all on "the first day of the week," Sunday, the day of Jesus' resurrection, that the Christians met "to break bread." ...Today we encounter [the celebration of the Eucharist] everywhere in the Church with the same fundamental structure. It remains the center of the Church's life.

CCC 1343

The Mass

Mrs. Evans led Lisa, Terrence, Tanya, and Tomás into the front pew of the church. Today they were attending their first Mass together.

Tanya looked around nervously. "I've never been to Mass before," she whispered to Lisa. "What if I do something wrong? How do I know what to do when?"

CCC 1341–1419

CHILDREN

The Mass

Read the story or ask a volunteer to read. Then ask the first reflection question to the class. To get honest answers, ask the children to shut their eyes and put their heads down and raise their hands if they would answer "yes" to this question.

Answer the second question as a group. Keep a list of all the things the children think of on the board.

Gather Together

Give the children time to answer the reflection question in their notebooks or prayer journals. Ask for volunteers to share their response.

Listen to God's Word

As you discuss this section with your group, ask the children if they have a favorite Bible story that they especially like listening to at Mass, or if they can remember a homily they especially liked.

Give the children time to answer the reflection questions, and ask for volunteers to share.

Are you ever nervous at Mass?

What would you tell Tanya to make her less afraid?

Gather Together

We come together in church for Mass to remember Jesus, "Do this in memory of me" (Luke 22:19) and because Jesus said, "Where two or three are gathered together in my name, there am I in the midst of them" (Matthew 18:20).

Mass begins with a gathering song. We sing together as the priest and ministers enter in a **procession**. The priest begins the celebration of the Mass by making the Sign of the Cross. This shows we all belong to God's family. He asks us to remember our sins. We ask God to forgive us.

Next, we sing or say the *Gloria*, an ancient Christian song of praise. We say, "Glory to God in the highest," just like the angels sang at Christmas. Then the priest says another short prayer.

What do you want to praise God for?

Listen to God's Word

Now we sit and listen to a reading from the Bible, God's word. This part of the Mass is called the **Liturgy of the Word**. The book of Mass readings is called a **Lectionary**. We hear three readings during Sunday Mass and two during weekday Mass.

In the first reading, we hear stories of God's love and mercy from the Old Testament. Then we sing the **Responsorial Psalm**. The psalms are prayer-poems that the Jewish people sing to God.

The second reading tells us how the early Church lived and prayed. After that reading, we stand and sing "Alleluia" before the final reading, the Gospel. *Alleluia* means "praise God" and *gospel* means "good news." So we praise God for his good news during this reading.

After the Gospel, the priest explains the readings in his homily. The **homily** teaches us what God's word means and how it applies to our lives today.

*How do you use words
to praise God?*

How can you praise God by listening?

Share and Pray

We share things about our lives with our families. We also ask our families for help when we're stuck or feeling bad. Our Church community is like a really big extended family. So during the **Universal Prayer** our Church family shares its concerns and problems, too. We pray together for our needs and the needs of others. We ask God to help and heal us. We hear requests, called **petitions**, and hold these prayers in our hearts.

*What do you want
to pray for today?*

Next, we get ready for the **Liturgy of the Eucharist**. *Eucharist* means "thanksgiving" and is another name for holy Communion. Just like your family gets together to share a meal, we share a meal at Mass with our Church family!

Before our meal, we bring gifts to God. This part of the Mass is called the **offertory** because we're offering things to God. The money placed into the basket helps the Church and the needy. The bread and wine that are carried to the altar become the Body and Blood of Jesus.

After receiving the bread and wine, the priest asks God to accept and bless these gifts in the **eucharistic prayer**. We praise God again with the *Holy, Holy, Holy*: "Holy, holy, holy, Lord God of hosts. Heaven and earth are full of your glory! Hosanna in the highest. Blessed is he who comes in the name of the Lord. Hosanna in the highest" (see Mark 11:7–11).

The priest, acting in the person of Jesus, says as Jesus said: "This is my body" and "this is my blood" (Mark 14:22, 24). We believe this is really Jesus in the bread and wine.

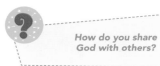

Join Together

We stand and pray the Our Father as one community in the Lord. As a tangible sign of the unity initiated by Christ, we say to those around us, "Peace be with you." We may also shake hands or hug each other.

Eat and Drink Together

We line up to receive the Eucharist, the true Body and Blood of Jesus Christ. When we eat this bread and drink this wine, Jesus' presence makes us more like him. After Communion, we silently thank God for coming to us.

After everyone has gone to Communion and after a final blessing, the Mass has ended. The priest says, "Go in peace." We reply, "Thanks be to God." We are proud to go out and share God with the world.

*How do you share
God with others?*

INQUIRY

JOURNEY OF FAITH

Join Together

As you go through this section, take time to pray the Our Father as a group and practice the sign of peace. Be sure to practice the conventions used in your parish so children will be familiar with what to do. For instance, do you hold hands during the Our Father or not? Do people usually raise their hands up or leave them folded?

Eat and Drink Together

Give the children time to answer the reflection question and ask for volunteers to share their answer.

Ask your group if anyone has questions over what happens at Mass that haven't been answered in the lesson. If you can't answer a question, write it down and find an answer by the next lesson.

69

Share and Pray

If you have time, create a list of petitions to use as your closing prayer today. You will want to include: a prayer for the Church and Church leaders (pray for the pope and the bishop of your diocese by name), the world and world leaders, your local community, your parish community, the sick (you may ask the children if they have anyone in particular they'd like to pray for, using first names only), those who have died, and special intentions.

Give the children time to write down a special intention in response to the reflection question. Remind them they won't have to share this intention if it's too personal.

Final Activity

Give the children time to complete the activity on their own. Walk around as children work and offer help if needed. Be sure to go over the correct answers (listed below) before the children leave.

If you have extra time or want to make this activity more active, once you have the Mass parts in order, go over what the children do during that part of Mass (sit, stand, kneel, shake hands, and so on).

3   Gloria

6   Our Father

4   Homily

2   Sign of the Cross

5   This is my Body

7   Sign of Peace

1   Gathering Song

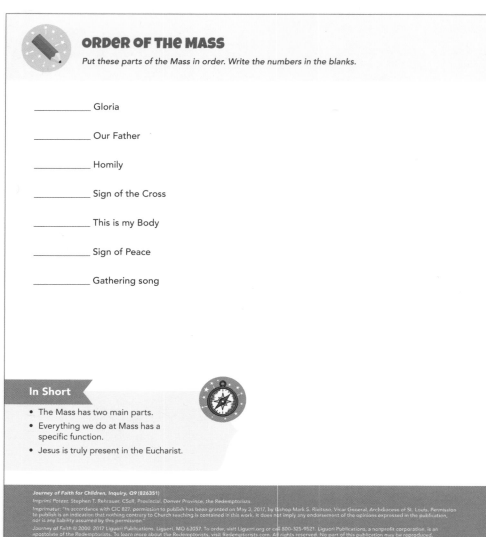

ORDER OF THE MASS

Put these parts of the Mass in order. Write the numbers in the blanks.

_____ Gloria

_____ Our Father

_____ Homily

_____ Sign of the Cross

_____ This is my Body

_____ Sign of Peace

_____ Gathering song

In Short

- The Mass has two main parts.
- Everything we do at Mass has a specific function.
- Jesus is truly present in the Eucharist.

Journey of Faith for Children, Inquiry, Q9 (826351)

Imprimi Potest: Stephen T. Rehrauer, CSsR, Provincial, Denver Province, the Redemptorists.

Imprimatur: "In accordance with CIC 827, permission to publish has been granted on May 3, 2017, by Bishop Mark S. Rivituso, Vicar General, Archdiocese of St. Louis. Permission to publish is an indication that nothing contrary to Church teaching is contained in this work. It does not imply any endorsement of the opinions expressed in the publication, nor is any liability assumed by this permission."

Journey of Faith © 2000, 2017 Liguori Publications, Liguori, MO 63057. To order, visit Liguori.org or call 800-325-9521. Liguori Publications, a nonprofit corporation, is an apostolate of the Redemptorists. To learn more about the Redemptorists, visit Redemptorists.com. All rights reserved. No part of this publication may be reproduced, distributed, stored, transmitted, or posted in any form by any means without prior written permission.

Editors of the 2017 Journey of Faith for Children: Theresa Nienaber-Panuski and Pat Fosarelli, MD, DMin.

Design and production: Wendy Barnes, Lorena Mitre Jimenez, John Krus, and Bill Townsend. Illustrations: Jeff Albrecht.

Unless noted, Scripture texts in this work are taken from the New American Bible, revised edition © 2010, 1991, 1986, 1970 Confraternity of Christian Doctrine, Washington, D.C., and are used by permission of the copyright owner. All Rights Reserved. No part of the New American Bible may be reproduced in any form without permission in writing from the copyright owner. Excerpts from the English translation of the Catechism of the Catholic Church for the United States of America © 1994 United States Catholic Conference, Inc.—Libreria Editrice Vaticana; English translation of the Catechism of the Catholic Church: Modifications from the Editio Typica © 1997 United States Catholic Conference, Inc.—Libreria Editrice Vaticana. Compliant with The Roman Missal, Third Edition.

Printed in the United States of America. 21 20 19 18 17 / 5 4 3 2 1. Third Edition.

Liguori PUBLICATIONS
A Redemptorist Ministry

Closing Prayer

Close with a reading of the petitions, either the ones you created during the lesson or the petitions that will be used next Sunday at Mass. Lead the children in the response, "Lord, hear our prayer." You can also finish with a recitation of the Lord's Prayer, which is prayed at every Mass.

Take-Home

Ask the children to pay close attention to the homily at Mass this week and come up with one question to ask their parents or sponsor or other adult who goes with them to Mass on the way home.

Q10: The Church Year

Catechism: 524–25, 1095, 1163–73, 1194–95

Objectives

- List the seasons of the Church year in the order they occur.
- Indicate which colors, symbols, and themes belong to what Church season.
- Name some feasts, holy days, and major saints celebrated during the liturgical year.

Leader Meditation

Ecclesiastes 3:1 and Mark 13:28–29

After reading these Scripture passages, reflect on the liturgical calendar and the framework and structure it offers for the expression of our faith, the sense of rhythm and rightness it brings to Church life, and the channel or passageway it provides for entering into the life, death, and resurrection of Christ for all the faithful.

Leader Preparation

- Read the lesson, this lesson plan, the Scripture passages, and the *Catechism* sections.
- Be familiar with the vocabulary terms for this lesson: Church year, Advent, Christmas, Lent, Triduum, Easter, Pentecost, Ordinary Time, feast days, holy days of obligation. Definitions are in this guide's glossary.
- Gather copies of a current liturgical chart or calendar for children and sponsors. Some parishes, organizations, and groups provide these free as Advent approaches, and others can be purchased year-round.

Welcome

Greet the children as they arrive. Check for supplies and immediate needs. Solicit questions or comments about the previous lesson and/or share new information and findings. Begin promptly.

Opening Scripture

Ecclesiastes 3:1 and Mark 13:28–29

Light the candle and read aloud. Suggest the children think about patterns or routines in their own lives. Before you begin today's lesson, ask the children if they've noticed anything about the church that changes from week to week or with the seasons.

If the children can't think of anything with just this question, prompt them by asking about the priest's vestments, colors used in decoration, flowers, altar cloths, or anything specific to your church that changes with the liturgical seasons.

> Once each week, on the day which she has called the Lord's Day, she keeps the memory of the Lord's resurrection....In the course of the year, moreover, she unfolds the whole mystery of Christ.
>
> CCC 1163

The Church Year

Lisa and Terrence were talking after Mass. "I wonder how the priest picks out what color robe to wear," Lisa said.

"He always seems to match the color of the church decorations," Terrence replied. "I wonder if they plan that."

"Maybe they share a calendar," Lisa said, giggling.

CCC 524–25, 1163–73, 1095, 1194–95

Celebrating With Family

Go around the room and ask each child to share one family tradition he or she has for the holidays, family game night, birthdays, or another special occasion. You can also share something your family did while you were growing up. Make sure everyone who wants to share has the chance, but don't spend too much time going off on tangents here.

Seasons of the Catholic Year

If you have liturgical calendars to hand out, do so now. Point out how you can easily see where each season starts by the colors of the day.

Ask the children if they can guess what colors Advent, Christmas, Lent, and Easter are without looking ahead in the lesson.

Advent

Ask the children to find the beginning of Advent on their liturgical calendar.

Two symbols of Advent are given in the lesson, but see if you can brainstorm more with the group. Encourage the children to write them down or draw pictures of them in their notebook.

Some additional symbols of Advent include the Advent wreath and the color pink.

Give the children time to answer the reflection questions on their own. Then ask them how they think the Church gets ready for Jesus during Advent.

Possible responses include decorating the church to let people know it's a special time, holding special Advent prayer services, lighting the Advent wreath during Mass, or spending extra time in prayer.

Christmas

Ask the children to find the beginning of Christmas on their liturgical calendar.

Give the children time to answer the reflection question on their own. Encourage them to think about more than just getting presents, which is really fun but shouldn't be the main event at Christmastime.

Lent

Ask the children to find the beginning of Lent on their liturgical calendar.

Answer the reflection question as a group and create a list of things the children can give up or add to their lives during Lent to be more like Jesus.

Some possible responses include sacrificing a food treat for forty days, giving up some of their free time to do extra chores, doing yard work for an elderly neighbor for free, getting up a few minutes early to say a special morning prayer to Jesus, or picking a saint to research and read about during Lent.

Celebrating With Family

All families have traditions. It might be an annual family reunion barbecue. Or a secret-Santa drawing for Christmas. Traditions are things your whole family shares. When you grow up, you'll probably pass on these traditions, too.

What traditions does your family have?

Seasons of the Catholic Year

The Church has traditions, too. In fact, the Church has a lot of traditions! To keep track of all the special Church celebrations, the Church has its own calendar. The **Church year** begins on the first Sunday of Advent. The Church year is organized to help us understand and experience all the Church traditions. Each season has its own special meanings, symbols, and colors.

Advent

Color: Violet, for humility and hope.

Symbols: Candles and stars represent Christ as the Way and the Light. Evergreen branches remind us of eternal life and Jesus' family tree.

Advent begins in late November or early December. During Advent, we look forward to the birth of Jesus at Christmas. We hear how God's people waited for a Savior in the readings at Mass. We hear about God's angel messengers and about John the Baptist, who prepared the way for Jesus.

How do you normally get ready for Christmas?

How can you prepare yourself for the coming of Jesus?

Christmas

Colors: White or gold, for light, innocence, and joy.

Symbols: Gifts represent the three gifts the Wise Men brought to Jesus. The star of Bethlehem reminds us that Christ shows us the way to him.

Christmas isn't just one day for Catholics. The Church's Christmas season begins on December 25 and continues into January! During Christmastime we hear about Jesus' birth. We learn about the three Wise Men who worshiped Baby Jesus. We also hear about Jesus' childhood, like how Mary and Joseph presented Jesus in the Temple. We also hear the story of Jesus' baptism.

What's your favorite part of celebrating Christmas?

Lent

Color: Purple, for sorrow and penance.

Symbols: Ashes remind us of our sins and God's mercy. The cross reminds us of Jesus' death. A crown of thorns reminds us of Jesus' suffering for us.

Lent begins on Ash Wednesday, which is in February or March. Lent lasts for forty days. We are supposed to spend these forty days getting ready for Easter. During Lent we reflect on everything Jesus has done for us. We pay special attention to his mercy, forgiveness, and suffering on the cross. We also try to do extra-good deeds to show our love. We can also give up something we like as a way of showing Jesus we are grateful for his sacrifice and want to be like him.

What could you do during Lent to show Jesus you want to be like him?

Triduum: The Last "Three Days"

Colors: On Holy Thursday and Holy Saturday we use white to represent Jesus' victory over death on Easter. On Good Friday we use red to represent Jesus' sacrifice for us.

Symbols: Candles represent Jesus, the Light of the World. We wash the feet of others to show that we will serve like Jesus. The cross reminds us of Jesus' sacrifice and death.

Lent ends in a three-day celebration called the **Triduum**. On Holy Thursday evening, we remember how Jesus shared the first Eucharist with his disciples by giving them his Body and his Blood. On Good Friday, we remember Jesus' crucifixion. On Holy Saturday at sunset, the Church celebrates Christ's resurrection at the Easter Vigil. During the Easter Vigil Mass you will receive the sacraments of initiation.

Easter

Colors: White or gold, for Christ is our Light, victory over death, and eternal glory.

Symbols: A lamb represents Jesus' sacrifice for us. Eggs represent our new life now that Jesus has risen from the dead.

The **Easter** season begins in March or April and lasts for fifty days. The last day of the Easter season is called **Pentecost**. During Easter we celebrate Jesus' resurrection and the news that we, too, will rise and live forever in heaven. We also remember how the Holy Spirit came to the apostles and made them strong, wise, and eager to build the Church. The Holy Spirit also comes to us through our baptism and confirmation.

How can you celebrate Jesus' victory over death?

Ordinary Time

Color: Green, for growth and eternal life.

Symbols: Plants, because they represent the growth that occurs during this time.

We celebrate **Ordinary Time** twice each year. The first time is between Christmas and Lent, usually January and February. It's celebrated again after Pentecost until Advent. During Ordinary Time, we learn about Jesus' travels, miracles, and teachings. The more we learn about our faith, the better we know and love God.

ACTIVITY
FEAST DAYS AND HOLY DAYS

These six seasons aren't the only things the Church year includes. It also suggests **feast days** for important events and saints. Some feast days are so special they are called **holy days of obligation**. That means we have to go to Mass, even if it's not a Sunday, to celebrate with the rest of our Church family.

In the United States, these are the holy days we celebrate:

- January 1: Mary, the Holy Mother of God
- Sixth Thursday or seventh Sunday of Easter: The Ascension of the Lord
- August 15: The Assumption of Mary, when her body was taken into heaven
- November 1: All Saints
- December 8: The Immaculate Conception of Mary
- December 25: The Nativity of the Lord (Christmas)

Have you ever celebrated one of these holy days?

Q10

Triduum: The Last "Three Days"

Ask the children to find the days of the Triduum on their liturgical calendar. You can use this to connect back to previous lessons by asking children where else the number three was important (your lesson on the Trinity).

Easter

Ask the children to find Easter on their liturgical calendar.

As you read through this section, remind children that this Easter will be very special to them because they'll be becoming full members of the Church!

Ordinary Time

Ask the children to find Ordinary Time on their liturgical calendar.

Feast Days and Holy Days

Ask the children to look for special feast days or holy days on their liturgical calendar. They can look for the ones listed in the lesson or try to find different feast days.

Final Activity

Give the children time at the end of the lesson to complete the final activity. Walk around as the children work and see how they're doing. Affirm correct answers and help clarify any points of confusion.

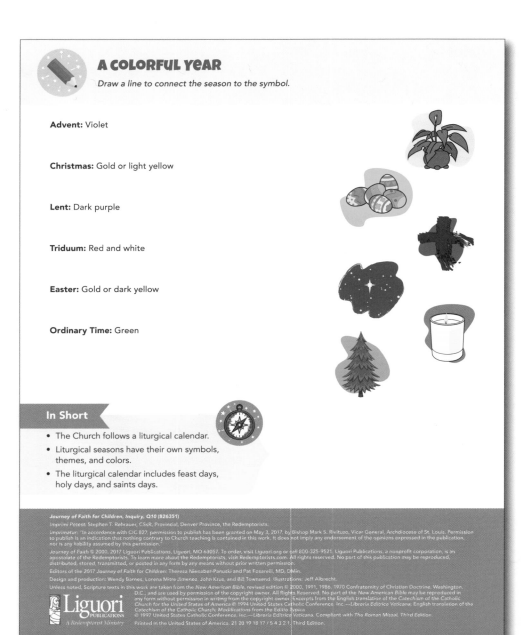

A COLORFUL YEAR

Draw a line to connect the season to the symbol.

Advent: Violet

Christmas: Gold or light yellow

Lent: Dark purple

Triduum: Red and white

Easter: Gold or dark yellow

Ordinary Time: Green

In Short

- The Church follows a liturgical calendar.
- Liturgical seasons have their own symbols, themes, and colors.
- The liturgical calendar includes feast days, holy days, and saints days.

Journey of Faith for Children, Inquiry, Q10 (826351)

Imprimi Potest: Stephen T. Rehrauer, CSsR, Provincial, Denver Province, the Redemptorists.

Imprimatur: "In accordance with CIC 827, permission to publish has been granted on May 3, 2017, by Bishop Mark S. Rivituso, Vicar General, Archdiocese of St. Louis. Permission to publish is an indication that nothing contrary to Church teaching is contained in this work. It does not imply any endorsement of the opinions expressed in the publication, nor is any liability assumed by this permission."

Journey of Faith © 2000, 2017 Liguori Publications, Liguori, MO 63057. To order, visit Liguori.org or call 800-325-9521. Liguori Publications, a nonprofit corporation, is an apostolate of the Redemptorists. To learn more about the Redemptorists, visit Redemptorists.com. All rights reserved. No part of this publication may be reproduced, distributed, stored, transmitted, or posted in any form by any means without prior written permission.

Editors of the 2017 *Journey of Faith for Children:* Theresa Nienaber-Panuski and Pat Fosarelli, MD, DMin.

Design and production: Wendy Barnes, Lorena Mitre Jimenez, John Krus, and Bill Townsend. Illustrations: Jeff Albrecht.

Unless noted, Scripture texts in this work are taken from the *New American Bible,* revised edition © 2000, 1991, 1986, 1970 Confraternity of Christian Doctrine, Washington, D.C., and are used by permission of the copyright owner. All Rights Reserved. No part of the *New American Bible* may be reproduced in any form without permission in writing from the copyright owner. Excerpts from the English translation of the *Catechism of the Catholic Church for the United States of America* © 1994 United States Catholic Conference, Inc. —Libreria Editrice Vaticana; English translation of the *Catechism of the Catholic Church: Modifications from the Editio Typica* © 1997 United States Catholic Conference, Inc.—Libreria Editrice Vaticana. Compliant with *The Roman Missal, Third Edition.*

Printed in the United States of America. 21 20 19 18 17 / 5 4 3 2 1. Third Edition.

Liguori PUBLICATIONS
A Redemptorist Ministry

Closing Prayer

Close with a spontaneous prayer thanking God for the gift of the Church Year (liturgical calendar), which unites the Church and deepens our faith, just as family gatherings and traditions become a bond among the members.

Take-Home

Ask the children to research feast days at home and choose one that celebrates an event or a saint they feel a connection to and put it on their calendar. Encourage them to do something special with their family on this day. It can be cooking a meal the saint might have eaten, saying a special prayer for that saint's intercession, or researching the feast day and sharing what they learned with their family.

Q11: Places in a Catholic Church

Catechism: 1179–86, 2179

Objectives

- Locate various places and objects within a typical parish church.
- Describe the various places and objects by function and significance.
- Discover that when we gather together in church, Christ is in our midst.

Leader Meditation

Psalm 84

Take your Bible to church when no formal rites are in progress, and kneel silently before the Lord for a few moments. Pray for the guidance and insight you need to instruct the young people in your care. Be aware of the different elements in the church. Meditate on the many ways these symbols have touched your life.

Leader Preparation

- Read the lesson, this lesson plan, the Scripture passage, and the *Catechism* sections.
- Ask the pastor or deacon to assist you in displaying the various vestments to the participants. If he isn't available, simply borrowing a few items will suffice.
- Schedule a tour of a church, sacristy, or chapel. Whether or not this replaces the formal session, provide participants with quiet time for prayer. If a group tour isn't available, encourage participants and sponsors to plan their own private visit to the church.
- Research the histories and missions of your parish. Consider gathering a list of websites and other relevant information for participants and sponsors interested in researching it further.
- Be familiar with the vocabulary terms for this lesson: holy water, baptismal font, genuflect, tabernacle, sanctuary lamp, pew, altar, *The Roman Missal*, crucifix, ambo, lectern, Easter candle, reconciliation room, confessional, vestments, sacristy, alb, stole, yoke, chasuble, parish, parish center, rectory. Definitions are in this guide's glossary.

Welcome

Greet the children as they arrive. Check for supplies and immediate needs. Solicit questions or comments about the previous lesson and/or share new information and findings. Begin promptly.

Opening Scripture

Psalm 84

If it's possible for this lesson, read aloud from the lectern. Talk about praying in church, the dwelling place of the Lord. Ask the children what they think it means for God to dwell in the church.

> Our visible churches, holy places, are images of the holy city, the heavenly Jerusalem toward which we are making our way on pilgrimage.
>
> CCC 1198

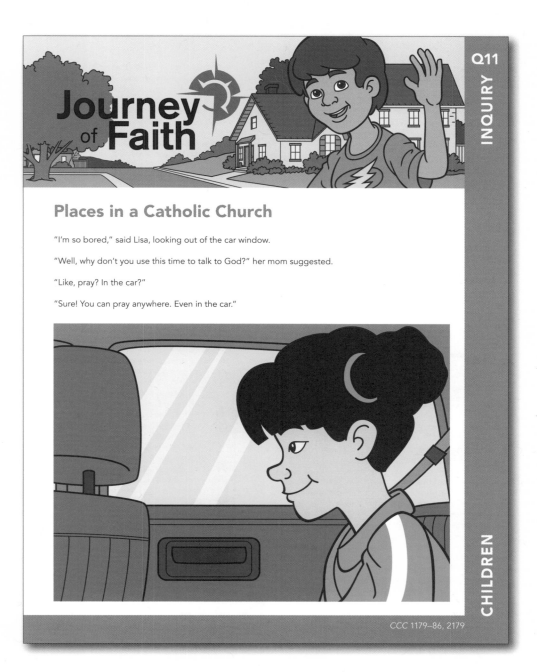

Places in a Catholic Church

"I'm so bored," said Lisa, looking out of the car window.

"Well, why don't you use this time to talk to God?" her mom suggested.

"Like, pray? In the car?"

"Sure! You can pray anywhere. Even in the car."

CCC 1179–86, 2179

Places in a Catholic Church

After reading the story for this lesson, ask the children to share one place they like to pray or the place they pray the best. You can start with volunteers but give every child the chance to respond.

What's What in the Church

As you talk about each place or thing in the church, show the children an example. You can do this by either going around to each thing where it is in your parish church or by having pictures of each item printed out or on a slide show.

You may also want to tie each item to its relevant sacrament (if it's connected to one). When you stop at the baptismal font, tell the children that those preparing for baptism will be baptized with this holy water (though not in the font itself). Show the children where the tabernacle is and, if you can, have a priest show them the consecrated host and let them know they'll be receiving this food at their first Eucharist.

If you're able, go inside the reconciliation room or confessional. Show the children where they'd kneel or sit and let them know they have the option to go behind the screen or face to face. Even some adults can be intimidated by going in the confessional, so help the children become familiar with it so they don't see it as scary later.

"I thought we had to be in church to pray," Lisa said.

"Nope," her mom said, shaking her head. "The church is just a very special place to pray. It's like going over to God's house to talk to him in person. It's also a place where we can pray with other people altogether."

Where do you like to pray?

What's What in the Church

You can pray anywhere. You can pray in the park. You can pray by your bed. You can pray with your family around the dinner table. God is everywhere, so he can hear you no matter where you are. Churches are special places where we pray and worship God. Everything you see in church is a reminder of how much God loves you.

When you walk in the church door, you'll see a small bowl of water. This bowl is filled with **holy water**. It's holy because it's water that's been blessed by a priest. You touch the water and make the Sign of the Cross. This is a reminder of your baptism in Jesus and your place in God's family.

You might also see a **baptismal font**. This is a large bowl or fountain of holy water used for baptizing new Christians.

When you come into the church, you **genuflect** toward the tabernacle. This means you briefly kneel with one knee on the floor and bless yourself with the Sign of the Cross. The **tabernacle** is the place where the Body of Jesus is kept, in the form of the Communion host. You genuflect toward the tabernacle to show respect for Jesus' presence in the church.

Near the tabernacle is a candle that burns at all times. This is the **sanctuary lamp**. It reminds us that Jesus is in the tabernacle and with us always.

Then you sit down on a wooden bench, called a **pew**. All the pews face toward the altar. The **altar** is where the priest offers the bread and wine to God and where the bread and wine are changed into the Body and Blood of Jesus. A book of Mass prayers is also used at the altar. This book is called *The Roman Missal*.

You will also see a crucifix above the altar. A **crucifix** is a cross with the image of Jesus on it. It is a reminder that Jesus loves us enough to suffer and die for us.

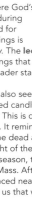

Usually in front of the altar and closer to the pews are an ambo and a lectern. An **ambo** is a stand where God's word is proclaimed during Mass. The book used for these Scripture readings is called the *Lectionary*. The **lectern** is another stand where we hear readings that aren't from Scripture or where the song leader stands.

You might also see a tall, white, decorated candle at the front of the church. This is called the **Easter candle**. It reminds us that Jesus rose from the dead at Easter time and is the Light of the World. During the Easter season, this candle burns at every Mass. After the Easter season it is placed near the baptismal font to remind us that we were baptized into Jesus' family and will rise with him one day.

Your church will also have a **reconciliation room** or **confessional**. This is where we go to talk to the priest about our sins. Here we are reminded of God's forgiving love and receive God's blessing.

Priests and Dressing for Church

The priest, deacon, and altar servers wear special clothing during Mass. This clothing is like the other things in the church, a reminder of our faith and how much God loves us. These articles of clothing are called **vestments**. Vestments are put on in the **sacristy**, a small room near the altar.

First, priests and deacons put on an **alb**, a long, white garment that reminds us we should approach God with purity of heart. The altar servers also wear albs.

Then the priest and deacon add a **stole**. This is a long piece of cloth to remind us of the yoke of the Lord. A **yoke** is used on farms. It is attached to a plow, which is pulled by an ox or other animal. So the stole is a sign that the one who wears it is doing hard work for God. The priest wears the stole straight down from the shoulders. The deacon wears the stole across one shoulder.

Over the alb and stole, the priest wears a **chasuble**, a sleeveless outer vestment. The colors of the chasuble represent the seasons of the church.

Other Buildings Near the Church

A church, its priest, and its people make up a **parish**. Parishes are named after the Trinity, Jesus, the Holy Spirit, Mary, or saints and important church feasts. The other buildings near the church are used to help run the parish. There is often a **parish center** where parish activities are held, like meetings and classes. The **rectory** is the house where the parish priest lives. Your parish may also have a school.

Priests and Dressing for Church

As you go through the vestments for a priest, you may also want to talk about the vestments altar servers wear. If it's possible, have an altar server who is close to the ages of your participants come and talk about what it's like to be an altar server. You could even take the names of any participants who think they might like to serve as an altar server and set up a meeting with the altar server coordinator at some point during your mystagogy lessons.

Other Buildings Near the Church

If it's open, walk the children through your parish center or just walk them over to the parish center.

Do the same for the rectory, but be sure to talk to your parish priests first so they'll be expecting you.

Final Activity

End your lesson back in the parish church and ask the children to complete the activity by finding the things themselves or with a partner. Remind the children that even when Mass isn't going on, God is present in the church building, so they should use the same respectful voices and behavior now as they would on Sunday at Mass.

 WHERE IS IT?

Find the following things in your church. Then draw a picture of each one under its name.

Holy water font

Altar

Crucifix

Tabernacle

Baptismal font

Sanctuary lamp

In Short

- Every place and object in the church carries a unique meaning.
- These things hold significance for the daily lives of Catholics.
- When we gather in church, Christ is with us.

Journey of Faith for Children, Inquiry, Q11 (826351)
Imprimi Potest: Stephen T. Rehrauer, CSsR, Provincial, Denver Province, the Redemptorists.
Imprimatur: "In accordance with CIC 827, permission to publish has been granted on May 3, 2017, by Bishop Mark S. Rivituso, Vicar General, Archdiocese of St. Louis. Permission to publish is an indication that nothing contrary to Church teaching is contained in this work. It does not imply any endorsement of the opinions expressed in the publication, nor is any liability assumed by this permission."
Journey of Faith © 2000, 2017 Liguori Publications, Liguori, MO 63057. To order, visit Liguori.org or call 800-325-9521. Liguori Publications, a nonprofit corporation, is an apostolate of the Redemptorists. To learn more about the Redemptorists, visit Redemptorists.com. All rights reserved. No part of this publication may be reproduced, distributed, stored, transmitted, or posted in any form by any means without prior written permission.
Editors of the 2017 *Journey of Faith for Children*: Theresa Nienaber-Panuski and Pat Fosarelli, MD, DMin.
Design and production: Wendy Barnes, Lorena Mitre Jimenez, John Krus, and Bill Townsend. Illustrations: Jeff Albrecht.
Unless noted, Scripture texts in this work are taken from the *New American Bible*, revised edition © 2000, 1991, 1986, 1970 Confraternity of Christian Doctrine, Washington, D.C., and are used by permission of the copyright owner. All Rights Reserved. No part of the *New American Bible* may be reproduced in any form without permission in writing from the copyright owner. Excerpts from the English translation of the *Catechism of the Catholic Church for the United States of America* © 1994 United States Catholic Conference, Inc.—*Libreria Editrice Vaticana*. English translation of the *Catechism of the Catholic Church: Modifications from the Editio Typica* © 1997 United States Catholic Conference, Inc.—*Libreria Editrice Vaticana*. Compliant with *The Roman Missal, Third Edition.*
Printed in the United States of America. 21 20 19 18 17 / 5 4 3 2 1. Third Edition.

Liguori
PUBLICATIONS
A Redemptorist Ministry

Closing Prayer

Ask for any special intentions and then pray together, asking the children to repeat each line after you:

Lord,
you have created us
to know you, love you,
and serve you.

Indeed, we are wonderfully made.

Thank you for the gift of this church
and for the objects and symbols
we encounter here
that bring us closer to you.

Amen.

Take-Home

The next time the children and their family attend Mass or go to church, ask the children to pick one item in the church and teach their family what they've learned about it.

Q12: Who Shepherds the Church?

Catechism: 871–945

Objectives

- Discover that Jesus Christ founded the Church.
- List the hierarchy of official leaders of the Church.
- Define the pope as the shepherd of the Church on earth.

Leader Meditation

Matthew 16:18–19

Read the passage, then reflect on its meaning with this prayer:

Lord, you have called me to this special purpose, to make your ways known to the young people in your flock. Help me to inspire in them a love for your Church, an obedience to your teachings, an understanding of their own call to serve, and a listening ear to those who have been chosen to lead them. Renew my respect for each member of your Church, clergy and lay. Clarify for me the importance of structure and leadership. I ask this in the name of your Son, Jesus, who stands forever as the head of your body, the Church. Amen.

Leader Preparation

- Read the lesson, this lesson plan, the Scripture passage, and the *Catechism* sections.

- Invite your pastor or parish ministry leaders to talk to participants about their roles in the parish. If your church has children specific ministries, like a children's choir, youth group, or altar servers, ask those coordinators to come speak or provide their contact information to the children and their sponsors.

- If available, collect a prayer card with the current pope's picture on it to distribute to the children.

- Be familiar with the vocabulary terms for this lesson: pope, bishop, diocese, archdiocese, archbishop, auxiliary bishop, cardinal, priest, pastor, associate pastor, deacon, religious order, brother, monk, monastery, sister, nun, convent, laity, lector, altar server, eucharistic minister, extraordinary minister of holy Communion, music minister, cantor, usher. Definitions are in this guide's glossary.

Welcome

Greet the children as they arrive. Check for supplies and immediate needs. Solicit questions or comments about the previous lesson and/or share new information and findings. Begin promptly.

Opening Scripture

Matthew 16:13–20

Light the candle and read aloud. Before you begin the lesson, ask the children what they think it means when Jesus says Peter is the rock upon which Christ will build his Church.

> In the Church there is diversity of ministry but unity of mission. To the apostles and their successors Christ has entrusted the office of teaching, sanctifying, and governing in his name and by his power.
>
> *CCC 873; see Decree on the Apostolate of the Laity, (Apostolicam Actuositatem), 2*

Who Shepherds the Church?

"Why'd we have two priests at Mass today?" asked Tanya.

"I think one was a deacon, not a priest," answered Tomás. "Mrs. Evans said we might even have a bishop for our confirmation."

"But how will we know who's who?"

CCC: 871–945

Who Shepherds the Church?

After you read the story, ask the children if they can think of anyone who works in their church or any jobs people in the church do. You can prompt discussion by asking the children to think about Sunday Mass and list all the jobs people do there. These include leading songs, proclaiming the readings, celebrating the Mass, carrying the cross in the procession, serving and assisting the priest, and others.

The Pope

Answer the reflection question as a class. If you have a picture of the current pope, show it to the group and see if they can guess who it is. If you have prayer cards with the pope's photo on them, pass those out now.

Bishops

Answer the reflection question as a class. If you can, pull up a map of your diocese to show the children what areas it covers.

Priests

If your pastor or another parish priest came to your lesson today, ask him to lead this section of the lesson and share some of his own favorite things about being a priest. Give the children time to ask him questions about being a priest.

If you are unable to have a priest speak to your class, be sure you let the children know the names of the pastor and any other priests who are assigned to your parish.

Do you know all the people who work in your church?

When you are baptized, you become a member of a family. Like any family, the Catholic Church has a lot of members. Every one of us has an important role and unique work to do. Jesus' work is to watch over the Church and to lead and guide all the members toward God.

Here are some members of the Church and the work they are called to do.

The Pope

Jesus chose twelve apostles to help him bring people to God. To one he said, "You are Peter, and upon this rock I will build my church" (Matthew 16:18). Peter worked with the other apostles to build the Christian Church around the world.

Peter's job is now done by his successor, the pope. The **pope** watches over and guides the Church in the world. Just like Peter worked with the apostles, the pope works with the bishops. The bishops are the successors of the other apostles.

Who is the pope now?

Bishops

A **bishop** is in charge of all the parishes in a city or area. This area is called a **diocese**. A large diocese is called an **archdiocese**. If you live in an archdiocese, your bishop is called an **archbishop**. For really large dioceses, the bishop may have an **auxiliary bishop**. *Auxiliary* means "helper."

Sometimes the pope chooses a bishop to become a **cardinal**. It's the job of the cardinals to vote for a new pope.

What diocese or archdiocese are you in?

Who is the bishop of your diocese or archdiocese?

Priests

The bishops can't take care of many parishes and people alone. **Priests** help bishops at individual parishes. A priest who is in charge of his own parish is called a **pastor**. That word comes from the Latin word for "shepherd." So a pastor is like your shepherd in faith. Large parishes might have an **associate pastor** who helps the pastor.

Not all priests are in charge of a parish. Some travel to faraway lands to spread the word of God. Others teach in schools. Some priests work with the poor, and some priests care for the sick.

Who is the pastor of your parish?

Are there other priests who work in your parish? Who are they?

Do you know any sisters or brothers? Who are they?

Do you know the names of any religious orders?

Deacons

A **deacon** helps priests by reading the Gospel or giving the homily at Mass, helping with the poor and sick in the parish, and a lot of other things. Although a deacon's ministry is more limited than a priest's, some of the things a deacon can do are: preach at Mass, baptize, and preside at weddings.

Who are the deacons in your parish?

Sisters and Brothers

Some people devote their lives to God in a special way by becoming part of a religious order. A **religious order** is a group of men or women who share a common mission (like preaching, teaching, praying, or serving the needy). They promise to always obey God and their community and to live simply without a lot of stuff.

Religious men are called **brothers** or **monks** and may live in a **monastery**. Religious women are called **sisters** or **nuns** and may live in a **convent**. Whether they live together or alone, they promise never to marry.

Laity

The largest part of the body of Christ is called the **laity**. The primary purpose of the laity is to bring Christ into their homes and workplaces. Ultimately, it is the job of the laity to work in transforming the world for Christ.

- **Lectors** proclaim the Bible readings from the *Lectionary* aloud at Mass.

- **Altar servers** assist the priest during Mass and other celebrations. They may carry a cross or a candle, hold the book of prayers, and even help prepare for Communion.

- **Extraordinary ministers of holy Communion**: They are named to administer the Eucharist after it has been "made sacred" by a priest or the person celebrating the Mass.

- **Music ministers** lead the singing and play instruments at Mass and other celebrations. A **cantor** is the lead singer.

- **Ushers** greet people before and after Mass, help them find a seat, and collect the offertory gifts. They might also assist with the Communion lines.

Deacons

If you're able to have a deacon come and speak to your class, let him lead this section of the lesson. Give the children time to ask him questions about being a deacon or about the difference between being a deacon and being a priest.

If you're unable to have a deacon speak to your class, be sure to let the children know the names of all the deacons in your parish (if you have any) and how to tell if someone at Mass is a priest or deacon.

Sisters and Brothers

Answer the reflection questions as a group. If you have any religious people in your parish who are willing to come and speak to your group, ask them to lead the lesson.

If you're unable to have any guest speakers for this section, show some pictures of religious men and women and name some of the more well-known religious orders, such as the Franciscans, Redemptorists, Jesuits, Sisters of Charity, Carmelites, or others that have a special connection to your parish.

Laity

If you have any guest speakers for this section, let them lead the discussion. If your parish has ministries led by children (like a children's choir or altar servers), you may want to find speakers who are the same age as or a little older than the children in your class. Seeing kids their own age participating in parish ministry is a great way to help the children feel welcomed and visualize themselves serving the parish, too.

Final Activity

Give the children time to complete this activity on their own. If you have had a lot of guest speakers during this lesson, you may not have time for the activity. If that's the case, ask the children to complete the activity at home or with their godparent or sponsor. Answers to the activity appear below.

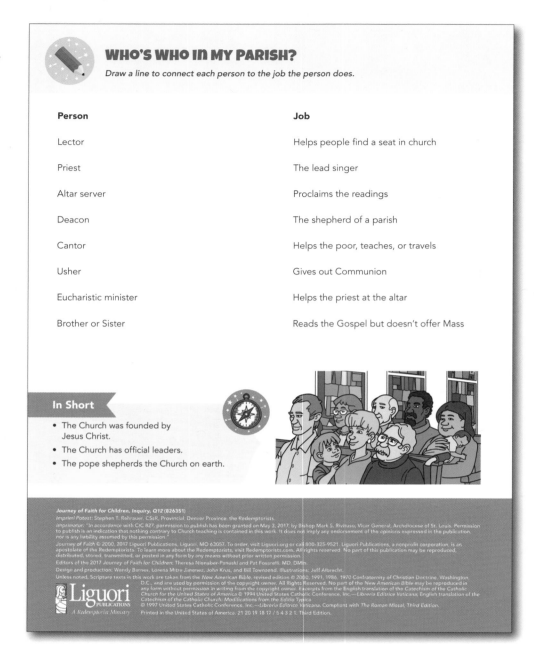

WHO'S WHO IN MY PARISH?

Draw a line to connect each person to the job the person does.

Person	Job
Lector	Helps people find a seat in church
Priest	The lead singer
Altar server	Proclaims the readings
Deacon	The shepherd of a parish
Cantor	Helps the poor, teaches, or travels
Usher	Gives out Communion
Eucharistic minister	Helps the priest at the altar
Brother or Sister	Reads the Gospel but doesn't offer Mass

In Short

- The Church was founded by Jesus Christ.
- The Church has official leaders.
- The pope shepherds the Church on earth.

Journey of Faith for Children, Inquiry, Q12 (826351)
Imprimi Potest: Stephen T. Rehrauer, CSsR, Provincial, Denver Province, the Redemptorists.
Imprimatur: "In accordance with CIC 827, permission to publish has been granted on May 3, 2017, by Bishop Mark S. Rivituso, Vicar General, Archdiocese of St. Louis. Permission to publish is an indication that nothing contrary to Church teaching is contained in this work. It does not imply any endorsement of the opinions expressed in the publication, nor is any liability assumed by this permission."
Journey of Faith © 2000, 2017 Liguori Publications, Liguori, MO 63057. To order, visit Liguori.org or call 800-325-9521. Liguori Publications, a nonprofit corporation, is an apostolate of the Redemptorists. To learn more about the Redemptorists, visit Redemptorists.com. All rights reserved. No part of this publication may be reproduced, distributed, stored, transmitted, or posted in any form by any means without prior written permission.
Editors of the 2017 *Journey of Faith for Children:* Theresa Nienaber-Panuski and Pat Fosarelli, MD, DMin.
Design and production: Wendy Barnes, Lorena Mitre Jimenez, John Krus, and Bill Townsend. Illustrations: Jeff Albrecht.
Unless noted, Scripture texts in this work are taken from the *New American Bible,* revised edition © 2010, 1991, 1986, 1970 Confraternity of Christian Doctrine, Washington, D.C., and are used by permission of the copyright owner. All Rights Reserved. No part of the *New American Bible* may be reproduced in any form without permission in writing from the copyright owner. Excerpts from the English translation of the *Catechism of the Catholic Church for the United States of America* © 1994 United States Catholic Conference, Inc.—*Libreria Editrice Vaticana;* English translation of the *Catechism of the Catholic Church: Modifications from the Editio Typica*
© 1997 United States Catholic Conference, Inc.—*Libreria Editrice Vaticana.* Compliant with *The Roman Missal, Third Edition.*
Printed in the United States of America. 21 20 19 18 17 / 5 4 3 2 1. Third Edition.

LIGUORI PUBLICATIONS
A Redemptorist Ministry

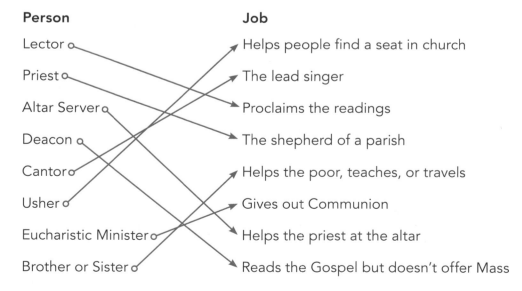

Person	Job
Lector	Helps people find a seat in church
Priest	The lead singer
Altar Server	Proclaims the readings
Deacon	The shepherd of a parish
Cantor	Helps the poor, teaches, or travels
Usher	Gives out Communion
Eucharistic Minister	Helps the priest at the altar
Brother or Sister	Reads the Gospel but doesn't offer Mass

Closing Prayer

You can be the leader (L) for this prayer, or ask a volunteer to read. The rest of the group will say the response (R) together.

L. For our pope, that he continues to lead the Church on earth. We pray to the Lord.

R. *Lord, hear our prayer.*

L. For our bishop, (Name), that he continues to lead our diocese closer to God.

R. *Lord, hear our prayer.*

L. For our parish priests, (Names), that they continue to shepherd our parish.

R. *Lord, hear our prayer.*

L. For our parish deacons, (Names), that they continue to assist in the work of the parish and spread the message of the Gospel.

R. *Lord, hear our prayer.*

L. For all religious men and women, that they continue to be Christ in the world.

R. *Lord, hear our prayer.*

L. For all those involved in lay parish ministry, especially in our parish, that they continue to be examples of service in the parish community.

R. *Lord, hear our prayer.*

Take-Home

Ask the children to take their lesson handout home today, if they don't normally, and lead the closing prayer with their family several times this week. Before dinner, before bed, or first thing in the morning are good times to suggest.

Q13: The Church as Community

Catechism: 74–95

Objectives

- Recognize that all Catholics are part of Christ's body.
- Discover that, in Christ, the Church possesses the fullness of truth.
- List some of the unique roles and duties held by Catholics in the Church.

Leader Meditation

John 14:15–31

The Church founded by Jesus Christ continues through the guidance and workings of the Holy Spirit, who dwells in every member. To understand the unity and power of the Church with its diverse membership, we must first believe that the Church is guided by the Holy Spirit, who works through Catholics everywhere. Though individuals make mistakes and are sometimes misguided, the people of God, as the Church, do not wander aimlessly.

Leader Preparation

- Read the lesson, this lesson plan, the Scripture passage, and the *Catechism* sections.
- Be familiar with the vocabulary term for this lesson: communion of saints. The definition is available in this guide's glossary.

Welcome

Greet the children as they arrive. Check for supplies and immediate needs. Solicit questions or comments about the previous lesson and/or share new information and findings. Begin promptly.

Opening Scripture

John 14:15–31

Light the candle and read the passage aloud. After reading, ask the children what we are to each other if our Father is God *(brothers and sisters)*. As the children think about this, explain how every member of the Church is part of our family. That is because we all have the same Father in God. This is what it means for the Church to be a community.

> The apostles entrust the "Sacred deposit" of the faith...to the whole of the Church. "By adhering to [this heritage] the entire holy people, united to its pastors, remains always faithful to the teaching of the apostles, to the brotherhood, to the breaking of bread and the prayers."
>
> *CCC 84*

The Church as Community

"A pop quiz?!" Lisa cried. "I thought this wasn't supposed to be like school!"

"I know," said Mrs. Evans. "But you won't be graded. I just want to see what you think makes a Church."

CCC 74–95

What Is the Church?

Give the children time to take the "quiz" on their own. Or if you prefer a more active variation, put letters A, B, and C on opposite walls. Read the question and answers out loud. Then ask the children to run under the letter that matches the answer they'd choose.

Jesus and His Church

While there are no correct or incorrect answers for this activity, for each question, "C" is the answer we can find in Scripture as Jesus built his Church. Go through each of the "C" answers and discuss why it's a Jesus response. Suggested responses appear below.

People. Jesus needs people to build his Church because without people there's no Church. Jesus came to die for us. He came to save us from our sins. He built his Church so people could continue to learn about his Father (in the Gospel), eat his bread and drink his blood (during holy Eucharist), and be forgiven (through reconciliation).

Gather your people. Jesus didn't want us to practice our faith in isolation. Whenever he preached, he preached to groups of people. He gathered people around him and commanded us to become servants of each other.

Teach your people to love one another. Jesus gave us the new commandment to love each other as we love ourselves. Loving other people as Jesus loves us is a cornerstone to being Catholic.

Place it in God's hands. Everything Jesus did he placed in the hands of his Father. When we get to know Jesus we learn about God the Father, too. Every person of the Trinity watches over our Church here on earth.

What do you think makes up a Church? Circle one answer for each question below and then share your answers with the group.

What Is the Church?

1. You are going to build a Church. What do you need to get started?

A. Bricks

B. Lots of money

C. People

2. What would you do first?

A. Hire a contractor

B. Dig a foundation

C. Gather your people

3. How can you be sure your Church will be strong?

A. Reinforce it with steel beams

B. Buy church insurance

C. Teach your people to love one another

4. What will you do to protect your Church?

A. Hire an armed guard

B. Build a wall around it

C. Place it in God's hands

5. How can you build a Church that will last forever?

A. Use super bricks

B. Hire a maintenance staff

C. Promise to be with your Church always

Jesus and His Church

If Jesus had answered these questions, he would have circled "C" every time.

Sometimes when we hear the word *church*, we think of a building filled with things that remind us of God. Or we think about the place we go to pray. That building is church with a lowercase "c." But the Church Jesus came to build was Church with a capital "C."

The True Meaning of Church

Jesus chose his apostles and taught them about God's love. He was preparing them to build the Church. When Jesus returned to heaven, the apostles started teaching others what Jesus taught them. They gathered people together to worship God. That's how they started the Church. The Church kept growing from there! God's word continues to be passed on today.

This is why the Church means more than a building. The Church is more than rules, even though some rules are necessary. The Church is more than the pope or bishops. The true meaning of *Church* is "people"; all the people who have faith in Jesus. The Church is a community of everyone who has been called to share God's life through Jesus.

Promise to be with your Church always. Just like Jesus placed the Church in his Father's hands, Jesus promised he would never leave us spiritually even if he wasn't with us physically. Jesus even sent us an advocate, the Holy Spirit, which we receive in a special way during our confirmation.

The True Meaning of Church

Give the children a couple of minutes to write a response to the reflection question. Then ask for volunteers to share their answers. This is a good opportunity for you to share some experiences of your own or let godparents and sponsors, share, too, if they're attending the lesson.

Sometimes, people call this community a family. That's because God is our Father, and we are all sisters and brothers in God's family. If we want to get to know our family, we have to spend time with them. It's the same with our Church family. We have to spend time getting to know the Church for our love to grow.

That's why we go to Mass on Sundays. It's like a big family meal. Everyone gets together, hears the same readings, participates in the same prayers, and shares the same heavenly meal.

How is your parish like a family?

The Body of Christ

Saint Paul had an interesting way of thinking about the community of Jesus' followers. In his First Letter to the Corinthians, he called the community "the body of Christ." Once Jesus ascended into heaven, he was no longer physically here on earth. That meant that his followers had to be his "body" on earth. We had to be the people who took care of others and loved them—just as Jesus did.

 Saint Paul said each of us is like a different part of the body. Some people are the hands of the Church. These people help those in need and do good works. Some people are the ears of the Church. These people listen to others with kindness. Some people are the brains of the Church. These people write books or help explain Church rules.

 A body needs all its parts to work well. Just like the body of Christ needs all of its people to really work in the world. We need each other, and everyone brings something new to the body of Christ. In fact, the Church even needs people who aren't with us on earth. All those souls in heaven or in purgatory are part of our Church, too. We call all the members of the Church—living, in purgatory, and in heaven—the **communion of saints**.

 God gives all of us gifts like special skills or talents. We're supposed to use these gifts to help build up the body. Someone with a beautiful voice might help the Church by singing in the choir. Someone who's really friendly might volunteer to be an usher. Someone else might be good at building things, so she or he might volunteer to help fix things around the church building.

What gifts did God give you?

The Body of Christ

Give the children a few minutes to respond to the reflection question. Encourage them to spend a minute in silent prayer asking for God's input on the question.

Final Activity

As you wrap up this lesson, save time for the children to complete the final activity on their own, or complete it as a group. Remind the children that, as members of Christ's body, the Church, we are all family. So if they have trouble coming up with an action for one of the prompts, they can think about ways they help or comfort members of their own families or their friends. A sample activity has been done below.

I am Jesus' hands when I *serve others by doing extra chores around the house or comfort others by giving a hug.*

I am Jesus' mouth when I *refuse to gossip about others and only say what is true and good.*

I am Jesus' heart when I *pray for others, show kindness to my classmates, and show love to my family.*

I am Jesus' feet when I *go out into the world and share my faith with others.*

I am Jesus' eyes when I *see other people as Jesus sees them, not how the world tells me to see them.*

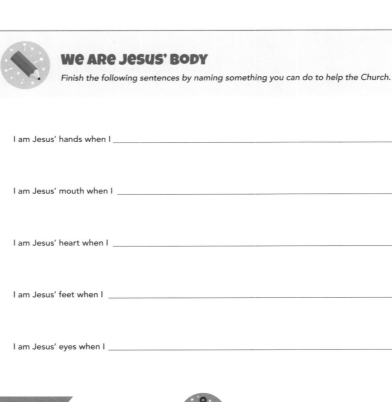

WE ARE JESUS' BODY

Finish the following sentences by naming something you can do to help the Church.

I am Jesus' hands when I _____.

I am Jesus' mouth when I _____.

I am Jesus' heart when I _____.

I am Jesus' feet when I _____.

I am Jesus' eyes when I _____.

In Short

- All Catholics are part of Christ's body.
- Catholics work together with unique roles and duties.
- In Christ, the Church possesses the fullness of truth.

Journey of Faith for Children, Inquiry, Q13 (826351)
Imprimi Potest: Stephen T. Rehrauer, CSsR, Provincial, Denver Province, the Redemptorists.
Imprimatur: "In accordance with CIC 827, permission to publish has been granted on May 3, 2017, by Bishop Mark S. Rivituso, Vicar General, Archdiocese of St. Louis. Permission to publish is an indication that nothing contrary to Church teaching is contained in this work. It does not imply any endorsement of the opinions expressed in the publication, nor is any liability assumed by this permission."
Journey of Faith © 2000, 2017 Liguori Publications, Liguori, MO 63057. To order, visit Liguori.org or call 800-325-9521. Liguori Publications, a nonprofit corporation, is an apostolate of the Redemptorists. To learn more about the Redemptorists, visit Redemptorists.com. All rights reserved. No part of this publication may be reproduced, distributed, stored, transmitted, or posted in any form by any means without prior written permission.
Editors of the 2017 Journey of Faith for Children: Theresa Nienaber-Panuski and Pat Fosarelli, MD, DMin.
Design and production: Wendy Barnes, Lorena Mitre Jimenez, John Krus, and Bill Townsend. Illustrations: Jeff Albrecht.
Unless noted, Scripture texts in this work are taken from the New American Bible, revised edition © 2000, 1991, 1986, 1970 Confraternity of Christian Doctrine, Washington, D.C., and are used by permission of the copyright owner. All Rights Reserved. No part of the New American Bible may be reproduced in any form without permission in writing from the copyright owner. Excerpts from the English translation of the Catechism of the Catholic Church for the United States of America © 1994 United States Catholic Conference, Inc.—Libreria Editrice Vaticana. English translation of the Catechism of the Catholic Church: Modifications from the Editio Typica © 1997 United States Catholic Conference, Inc.—Libreria Editrice Vaticana. Compliant with The Roman Missal, Third Edition.
Printed in the United States of America. 21 20 19 18 17 / 5 4 3 2 1. Third Edition.

Liguori PUBLICATIONS
A Redemptorist Ministry

Closing Prayer

Ask the children if they have any special intentions for today. If you haven't already taught the children how to share and respond to a petition (using the call and response "we pray to the Lord" and "Lord, hear our prayer"), this is a good time to begin practicing this tradition.

Take-Home

Ask the children to pick one action from the final activity that they can do with their family this week.

Q14: Mary

Catechism: 963–72

Objectives

- Discover Mary is the Mother of God and our Mother.
- Begin to describe the strong connection between Jesus and Mary.
- List some of Mary's different titles and explain what they tell us about her.

Leader Meditation

Luke 1:46–55

Reflect on the reading by praying the following prayer.

Lord, may my life magnify your presence here on earth. Like Mary, may I serve your people with humility and compassion. Like a loving mother or father, may I love and respect the young people in my care, accepting them for who they are. May I teach with patience and understanding. Amen.

Leader Preparation

- Read the lesson, this lesson plan, the Scripture passage, and the *Catechism* sections.
- If you have any resources on Mary you'd like to share with the children, organize those. *These can include books, prayer cards, information on Marian icons or apparitions, or information on churches or shrines dedicated to Mary.*
- Try to find a version of John Michael Talbot's song "Holy Is His Name" for the closing prayer.

Welcome

Greet the children as they arrive. Check for supplies and immediate needs. Solicit questions or comments about the previous lesson and/or share new information and findings. Begin promptly.

Opening Scripture

Luke 1:46–55

Light the candle and read the passage aloud. Explain that this passage is known as Mary's Magnificat. In this passage, the word *magnifies* means "glorifies." Ask the children how Mary glorifies God in this prayer. Responses may include sentences like:

She praises the greatness of the Lord.

God has done great things for her.

God is mighty and has thrown down rulers.

God has helped his servant, Israel.

> Mary's role in the Church is inseparable from her union with Christ and flows directly from it. "This union of the mother with the Son in the work of salvation is made manifest from the time of Christ's virginal conception up to his death."
>
> *CCC 964*

Mary

Mrs. Evans said that the next RCIA class would be "parents day" for moms and dads to see what they were learning.

"But I don't live with my mom," Lisa said, confiding in Tomás. "I have a stepmom instead."

"My grandmother takes care of me," Tomás said.

Mrs. Evans overheard them. "That's OK," she said. "Lots of different people can be our mothers. In fact, you even have a special mother in heaven. Her name is Mary."

CCC 963-72

Mothers Are Special

After reading this section, create a list or a word web of characteristics that make up what it means to be a mother in the context of this section.

Some words include: caring, compassionate, listening, thoughtful, gentle, joyful, happy, prayerful, strong, brave, and so on.

Prayerful

As you discuss this section, ask the children to think about a time they had to do something they were scared to do, like give a presentation at school or perform a solo but said, "yes," anyway. While Mary's decision was bigger than our everyday yeses, she was still afraid like us.

Give the children a few minutes to answer the reflection questions on their own. Ask for volunteers to share their response.

Mary was probably scared. She might have been humbled or confused about why God would have chosen her.

We might be scared to see an angel up close. Or even excited to see an angel. We might feel unworthy at first but then grateful that God has chosen us. We might feel courageous, knowing that God believes in us.

INQUIRY

JOURNEY OF FAITH

Mothers Are Special

Being a mother is a special job. Sometimes our "mother" isn't our biological mom. Or we might be "mothered" by our mom and other people. Fathers, grandmothers, aunts, big sisters, or even our friends' moms can be like our mother. Mothers are people who take care of you and love you. You can go to them when you need them.

We learn about Jesus' mother, Mary, in the Bible. Mary was the young girl God selected to be the Mother of God on earth. Each Bible story about Mary tells us something special about her.

Prayerful

The angel Gabriel appeared to Mary. "Hail Mary," Gabriel said. "You are truly blessed."

Gabriel could tell that Mary was afraid. "Don't be afraid," he said. "God loves you very much. You will have a son. His name will be Jesus. He will be called the Son of God." Mary was confused. "How can I have a baby? I'm not yet living with my husband," she said. The angel told her, "Nothing is impossible for God."

Mary loved God very much. "Let it happen as you have said," Mary said in agreement.

Read more about the angel's visit in Luke 1:26–38.

 How do you think Mary felt when the angel came to visit her?

How would you feel?

Helpful

The angel also told Mary her relative Elizabeth would be having a baby boy, too. Mary knew Elizabeth would need her help. So Mary went to visit Elizabeth and stayed with her for three months.

In Luke 1:39–56, read about Mary's visit to Elizabeth.

? *What can you do to be helpful like Mary?*

Humble

Just before Jesus was born, Mary went with Joseph, her husband, to Bethlehem for the census. This was because the king wanted to know how many people lived in his kingdom and where they lived. Going to Bethlehem was a long and difficult journey for Mary.

There was no place for them to stay in Bethlehem, so Mary gave birth to her baby in a stable for animals. Mary didn't mind. She was so happy to hold Jesus for the first time.

Read about humility in Luke 2:1–21.

? *Do you think it was hard for Mary to have her baby in a stable? Why?*

Helpful

Read Luke 1:39–56 aloud to the group or ask a volunteer or volunteers to read.

As a group, create a list of possible answers to the reflection question.

We can be helpful like Mary by helping our younger siblings or doing extra chores around the house to help our own family.

Humble

Read Luke 2:1–21 aloud to the group, or ask a volunteer or volunteers to read.

Give the children a couple of minutes to think about the reflection question on their own, then discuss as a group.

Brave

When Jesus was born, an angel appeared to Joseph. The angel told him the baby was in danger. King Herod was afraid Jesus would grow up and take away his kingdom. So King Herod wanted to kill Jesus.

The angel told Joseph to take Jesus and Mary to Egypt. Mary and Joseph had never been to Egypt before. But they trusted God. So Joseph, Mary, and Jesus went to Egypt and stayed there until God told them it was safe to go home.

Read about their bravery in Matthew 2.

Have you ever moved to a new place? Was it scary?

How do you think Mary and Joseph felt about leaving home?

Caring

As Jesus grew up, he did a lot of things with his mom. Once, at a wedding in Cana, Mary saw that the wedding party had run out of wine. She was sad that their celebration would be ruined. She told Jesus about the problem.

Jesus took six stone jars filled with water and blessed them. The water became wine. Everyone was amazed. Jesus performed this first miracle because Mary cared so much.

Read about the miracle in John 2:1–12.

Have you ever done something because someone believed in you?

Faithful

After Jesus died on the cross, his disciples were scared. They were worried people would want to kill them, too. So they ran away. But Mary didn't run away. Mary stayed by Jesus. She didn't leave him even though it was hard for her to watch him die. Jesus loved his mother, too. He asked his "beloved disciple" to take care of her.

Read about faithfulness in John 19:25–27.

Do you think you would have stayed by Jesus?

Mary in Heaven

Today Mary is in heaven with Jesus. She watches over all of God's children just like she watched over Jesus. Mary watches over us by listening to our prayers and sharing our prayers with God. Anytime you need help, you can ask Mary to pray for you and look out for you.

When we pray to Mary, we aren't worshiping her. We only worship God. We pray to Mary because she is very close to God. We honor Mary for the life she lived and because she was Jesus' mother. We try to imitate Mary because she lived her life so close to God, and we want to be close to God, too.

Brave

Read Matthew 2 aloud to the group or ask a volunteer or volunteers to read.

Ask the children to respond to the reflection questions on their own or ask the children to find a partner and talk about their answers with each other.

Caring

Read John 2:1–12 aloud to the group or ask a volunteer or volunteers to read.

Give the children time to answer the reflection questions on their own.

Faithful

Read John 19:25–27 aloud to the group or ask a volunteer or volunteers to read.

Give the children time to answer the reflection questions on their own.

WHAT MAKES A MOTHER?

The words below describe a mother. Unscramble each word and then unscramble the starred letters to solve for the hidden word.

LUFFATHI _____ _____ _____ _____ _____ _____ _____ _____

EBARV _____ ★ _____ _____ _____ _____

LHEPLUF _____ _____ _____ _____ _____ _____ _____

MUHLBE _____ _____ _____ ★ _____ _____

ACRGNI _____ _____ ★ _____ _____ _____

YARREPLUF _____ _____ _____ _____ ★ _____ _____ _____

The hidden word is: _____ _____ _____ _____

In Short

- Mary is the Mother of God and our Mother.
- Mary and Jesus share a strong connection.
- Mary's different titles share who she is to us.

Journey of Faith for Children, Inquiry, Q14 (826351)
Imprimi Potest: Stephen T. Rehrauer, CSsR, Provincial, Denver Province, the Redemptorists.
Imprimatur: "In accordance with CIC 827, permission to publish has been granted on May 3, 2017, by Bishop Mark S. Rivituso, Vicar General, Archdiocese of St. Louis. Permission to publish is an indication that nothing contrary to Church teaching is contained in this work. It does not imply any endorsement of the opinions expressed in the publication, nor is any liability assumed by this permission."
Journey of Faith © 2000, 2017 Liguori Publications, Liguori, MO 63057. To order, visit Liguori.org or call 800-325-9521. Liguori Publications, a nonprofit corporation, is an apostolate of the Redemptorists. To learn more about the Redemptorists, visit Redemptorists.com. All rights reserved. No part of this publication may be reproduced, distributed, stored, transmitted, or posted in any form by any means without prior written permission.
Editors of the 2017 *Journey of Faith for Children*: Theresa Nienaber-Psauski and Pat Fosarelli, MD, DMin.
Design and production: Wendy Barnes, Lorena Mitre Jimenez, John Krus, and Bill Townsend. Illustrations: Jeff Albrecht.
Unless noted, Scripture texts in this work are taken from the *New American Bible*, revised edition © 2000, 1991, 1986, 1970 Confraternity of Christian Doctrine, Washington, D.C., and are used by permission of the copyright owner. All Rights Reserved. No part of the *New American Bible* may be reproduced in any form without permission in writing from the copyright owner. Excerpts from the English translation of the *Catechism of the Catholic Church for the United States of America* © 1994 United States Catholic Conference, Inc.—*Libreria Editrice Vaticana*; English translation of the *Catechism of the Catholic Church: Modifications from the Editio Typica* © 1997 United States Catholic Conference, Inc.—*Libreria Editrice Vaticana*. Compliant with *The Roman Missal, Third Edition*.
Printed in the United States of America. 21 20 19 18 17 / 5 4 3 2 1. Third Edition.

Liguori PUBLICATIONS
A Redemptorist Ministry

Final Activity

As you wrap up this lesson, save time for the children to complete the "What Makes a Mother" final activity on their own. If they need help unscrambling a word, encourage them to look back through the lesson handout. Answers appear below.

LUFFATHI F A I T H F U L

EBARV B **R** A V E

LHEPLUF H E L P F U L

MUHLBE H U **M** B L E

ACRGNI C **A** R I N G

YARREPLUF P R A **Y** E R F U L

The hidden word is: **M A R Y**

Closing Prayer

Dim the lights and listen to the words of Mary's Magnificat in John Michael Talbot's song "Holy Is His Name." If the song is unavailable, pray the Hail Mary.

Take-Home

This week, ask the children to lead the Hail Mary as a family prayer before meals.

Q15: The Saints

Catechism: 946–59, 2683–84

Objectives

- Define canonization as the official process to become a saint.
- Discover that the saints weren't always perfect.
- Describe the saints as members of the Church who help us from heaven.

Leader Meditation

Prayer

Lord Jesus, I remember your promise, "I will not leave you orphans." You have sent your Holy Spirit to be with us, to guide us, to lead us to heaven. All who are filled with your Spirit are with us in the communion of saints. Grant that I may always recognize their presence and be guided toward holiness by their example. Help me to encourage the young people in my care to seek out and follow those you have sent to teach us and to lead us. Amen.

Leader Preparation

- Read the lesson, this lesson plan, and the *Catechism* sections.
- Collect any books or other resources on the lives of the saints (such as *Butler's Lives of the Saints*) that will be useful for the lesson, the activity, or just for show and tell. Liguori's *The Saints and Me* series is another good resource and perfect for children. You may consider getting a special book for each child or a class set to use as a resource.
- Research saints that share the names of each child in your class. Write this name on a note card or a sticky note to hand to each child. You could also use nametags.
- Be familiar with the vocabulary terms for this lesson: saint, canonization, patron saints, seminary. Definitions can be found in this guide's glossary.

Welcome

Greet the children as they arrive. Check for supplies and immediate needs. Solicit questions or comments about the previous lesson and/or share new information and findings. Begin promptly.

Opening Story

Instead of a reading from Scripture, choose a story from the lives of the saints. Light the candle and read the story of this special saint to the group. Pick a younger saint to help the children apply the story to their own lives. Then ask the children what stood out to them in the story they just read or heard.

> The witnesses who have preceded us into the kingdom, especially those whom the Church recognizes as saints, share in the living tradition of prayer by the example of their lives, the transmission of their writings, and their prayer today.
>
> *CCC 2683*

The Saints

"When I get bigger I'm gonna be able to run really fast. Just like my favorite athletes," Terrence said.

"I wanna be able to sink baskets from the three-point line!" Tomás said, jumping up in the air and pretending to shoot a basket.

"I've got posters of all my favorite players up in my room. Then I can look at them and remind myself why I need to practice! I'm getting pretty good," Terrence said, smiling.

CCC 946–59; 2683–84

The Saints

After reading the story, give the children time to answer the reflection questions on their own.

Choose Your Heroes

As you begin this section, give the children a few minutes to name someone they consider a hero and why. The hero doesn't have to be a religious figure.

Give the children time to complete the reflection question on their own. Then go around the room and have each child share one of their characteristics of what it means to be a saint. List them somewhere everyone can see.

What are you trying to get really good at?
How do you practice?

God has a team of special "athletes," too. They learned all about God. They followed Jesus' example. They studied the lives of other holy people. Sometimes they made mistakes. They weren't born perfect and holy. But they all loved God. So they kept practicing. We call these holy athletes **saints**.

What does the word saint mean to you?

When the Church names someone a saint, it's called canonization. **Canonization** is the Church's way of officially declaring that someone has lived such a holy life that he or she is certainly in heaven with God. You can read about saints in books and study their lives.

The Church doesn't know about every saint. You might have a saint living next door! You might even be related to a saint. These living saints are people who love God, believe in Jesus, and live holy, loving, and generous lives every day.

Do you know someone who might be a saint? Who?

Choose Your Heroes

Do you like to watch the Olympics? Do you have a favorite athlete or sport?

Athletes aren't born great at their sport. They spend years learning and practicing. They may read about other athletes. They practice. It takes a lot of practice to get ready for the Olympics.

To get ready, athletes follow the examples of other great athletes. They watch videos of the game. They study all the moves. They correct their mistakes. Then they practice some more. If you want to be great at something, you do the same thing. First, you learn how to play the game. Then you learn about the people who do it best. Then you practice until you get better. Then you practice some more.

Saints Help Us From Heaven

Canonized saints have feast days. A feast day is a special day of the year set aside to celebrate the life of a particular saint. For example, St. Francis of Assisi's feast day is October 4. Saint Mary Magdalene's feast day is July 22.

On a saint's feast day, or any other day of the year, we ask that saint to help us live a holy life. Some saints are called **patron saints** of something or a group of people. We can pray to these saints for special help. We might pray to St. Thomas Aquinas for help with a test because he's the patron saint of students.

Some people are named after saints. Are you? You can look up your name online or in a book like *Lives of the Saints* to see which saints share your name.

Do you share your name with a saint?

What patron saint would you like to pray to?

Some Saints to Know

St. Thérèse of Lisieux:
The Little Flower of Jesus
As a child, Thérèse wanted to serve God. Thérèse became a nun and lived in a convent. Her life in the convent wasn't always easy. Sometimes the other nuns were mean to her. But Thérèse was never mean back. In fact, she did small acts of kindness for others every day.

St. John Bosco:
Patron of Orphans
When John Bosco was sixteen, he entered the **seminary**, a special school for boys who want to become priests. There were a lot of poor, homeless, and orphaned children near the seminary. John wanted to help them. He took them into his own home, fed them, and taught them to love God. He became the father to hundreds of orphans who had been forgotten by the world.

St. Dominic Savio:
Patron of Choir Members
Even when he was only twelve, Dominic always knew when people needed help. He helped the poor and the homeless. He formed the Company of the Immaculate Conception, a group of boys who lived at St. John Bosco's house and helped take care of the orphans. Dominic died when he was only fifteen, but he spent all his time on earth serving others.

YOU CAN BE A SAINT, TOO!

- Learn as much as you can about God and holiness.
- Listen to Jesus' teachings and follow his example.
- Read about saints' lives to discover what makes them great.
- Imitate the living saints you know.
- Pray for God's help.
- Ask your favorite saint to pray with you.

Saints Help Us From Heaven

Discuss the first reflection question as a group by having people who know they share their name with a saint raise their hand. If you have a small enough group or enough time, you can let each child know of a saint they share their name with. If you prepared note cards for each child, pass those out now.

Let the children answer the second reflection question on their own.

Go around the room and see what the children are writing. Keep in mind any repeated answers and find a patron saint to share before your next lesson.

Some Saints to Know

Read about each of the saints listed here. If you have more time, you may want to read more about the saints than what's covered here. See "Leader Preparation" for some suggested books.

Final Activity

If you run out of time, the reading activity just noted is a perfect one for the children to research at home, especially if they'll need to choose a confirmation name. If you will have time for the students to complete the activity in class, have books about the saints available for them to use to research new saints.

PATRON SAINTS

Who is your patron saint? Write his or her name in the box below. If you can, find a picture of your saint and paste it in the box. If you can't find a picture, you can draw one!

Think about the saints you know. They can be canonized saints or living saints. For each category below, name one you would award a gold medal to. Under each name, write why you think that particular saint deserves a gold medal.

Gold Medal for Acts of Kindness:

Gold Medal for Listening to God:

Gold Medal for Forgiveness:

In Short

- Canonization is the official process the Church uses to name someone a saint.
- The saints weren't always perfect.
- The saints help us from heaven.

Journey of Faith for Children, Inquiry, Q15 (826351)
Imprimi Potest: Stephen T. Rehrauer, CSsR, Provincial, Denver Province, the Redemptorists.
Imprimatur: "In accordance with CIC 827, permission to publish has been granted on May 3, 2017, by Bishop Mark S. Rivituso, Vicar General, Archdiocese of St. Louis. Permission to publish is an indication that nothing contrary to Church teaching is contained in this work. It does not imply any endorsement of the opinions expressed in the publication, nor is any liability assumed by this permission."
Journey of Faith © 2000, 2017 Liguori Publications, Liguori, MO 63057. To order, visit Liguori.org or call 800-325-9521. Liguori Publications, a nonprofit corporation, is an apostolate of the Redemptorists. To learn more about the Redemptorists, visit Redemptorists.com. All rights reserved. No part of this publication may be reproduced, distributed, stored, transmitted, or posted in any form by any means without prior written permission.
Editors of the 2017 *Journey of Faith for Children*: Theresa Nienaber-Panuski and Pat Fosarelli, MD, DMin.
Design and production: Wendy Barnes, Lorena Mitre Jimenez, John Krus, and Bill Townsend. Illustrations: Jeff Albrecht.
Unless noted, Scripture texts in this work are taken from the *New American Bible*, revised edition © 2000, 1991, 1986, 1970 Confraternity of Christian Doctrine, Washington, D.C., and are used by permission of the copyright owner. All Rights Reserved. No part of the *New American Bible* may be reproduced in any form without permission in writing from the copyright owner. Excerpts from the English translation of the *Catechism of the Catholic Church for the United States of America* © 1994 United States Catholic Conference, Inc.—Libreria Editrice Vaticana; English translation of the *Catechism of the Catholic Church: Modifications from the Editio Typica* © 1997 United States Catholic Conference, Inc.—Libreria Editrice Vaticana. Compliant with *The Roman Missal, Third Edition.*
Printed in the United States of America. 21 20 19 18 17 / 5 4 3 2 1. Third Edition.

Liguori PUBLICATIONS
A Redemptorist Ministry

Closing Prayer

Choose a prayer written by the saint you read about in the "Opening Scripture" section. If you can't find one, you can pray this prayer by St. Thérèse of Lisieux, "The Little Flower," or take prayer suggestions from the group.

But how shall I show my love, since love proves itself by deeds?....The only way I have of proving my love is to strew flowers before Thee— that is to say, I will let no tiny sacrifice pass, no look, no word. I wish to profit by the smallest actions, and to do them for Love. I wish to suffer for Love's sake, and for Love's sake even to rejoice: thus shall I strew flowers.

Take-Home

Ask the children to research a saint with their parents this week. Encourage them to really get into their research by praying the saint's favorite prayers or cooking a food from the saint's home country.

Q16: What's Life After Death?

Catechism: 675–82, 988–1001, 1020–65

Objectives

- Distinguish between heaven and hell as the only two eternal outcomes.
- Define purgatory as a final purification in preparation for heaven.
- Begin to differentiate between particular judgment and the Final Judgment.

Leader Meditation

Luke 18:8

As you prepare for this lesson, do your own examination of conscience and assess where you are on the journey of becoming "holy as he is holy" so as to inherit eternal life.

Leader Preparation

- Read the lesson, this lesson plan, and the *Catechism* sections. This may help you answer questions about Catholic teaching on the rapture or other variations of the "end times."
- Gather art supplies and extra paper for the final activity.
- Be familiar with the vocabulary terms for this lesson: particular judgment, heaven, hell, purgatory, Final Judgment. Definitions can be found in this guide's glossary.

Welcome

Greet the children as they arrive. Check for supplies and immediate needs. Solicit questions or comments about the previous lesson and/or share new information and findings. Begin promptly.

Opening Scripture

Luke 18:8

Light the candle and read aloud. Following the reading, allow a moment of silence, then welcome comments or questions. Before beginning your discussion of the lesson handout, ask the participants what they think "justice" or a "just decision" means.

> Christ is Lord of eternal life. Full right to pass definitive judgment on the works and hearts of men belongs to him as redeemer of the world.
>
> *CCC 679*

Journey of Faith

What's Life After Death?

"What happens when we die?" Tanya asked. "Do we only get to go to heaven with other Catholics? What about people who don't believe in anything? Or people who do bad things?"

"Those are some serious questions," Mrs. Evans replied. "No one knows exactly what happens when we die. But the Church has information that can help us prepare and teaches us what eternal life will be like."

CCC 675–82; 988–1001; 1020–65

What's Life After Death?

After you read today's story, give the children time to answer the reflection question. They can write their response or draw a picture of heaven on a separate sheet of paper. Ask for volunteers to share their pictures or responses.

What Happens When Someone Dies?

Look at the vocabulary term "particular judgment" and ask children what "particular" means. Then ask them to put that definition together with their definition of "just decision" from the "Opening Scripture" question to create a class definition of "particular judgment." Clarify any misunderstanding as you read through the section.

If you want to continue the conversation, you can also ask the children what they think is different between God's judgment and human judgment here on earth.

God's judgment is always just. God knows everything, including our inner thoughts and motivations. Human judgment isn't always made in the best interest of everyone. Humans can't know other people's thoughts or judgment. However, because God gives us grace to accept the virtue of right judgment, some judgments about right and wrong can be just and right.

As you discuss the three outcomes of particular judgment, emphasize that a person only goes to hell if she or he rejects God outright. We don't go to hell for accidents or making mistakes we are truly sorry for and receive forgiveness for in reconciliation.

What kind of place do you think heaven is?

What Happens When Someone Dies?

Death can be sad, even scary, but Jesus helps us face death with courage. Jesus overcame death when he rose from the dead on the first Easter. He wants us to trust in the gift of eternal life we receive at baptism.

After death comes our **particular judgment**. This is when God reviews our life. God judges if we accepted and shared his gifts of love and mercy. We receive God's love by believing in him, loving him, and caring for others.

After our particular judgment there are three things that might happen:

1. We get to go straight to heaven.
2. We go to purgatory to get ready for our entrance into heaven.
3. We reject God and go to hell.

What Is Heaven?

Heaven is total, complete, "ultimate…happiness" (*CCC* 1024). In heaven, we joyously celebrate being one with the Father, Son, Holy Spirit, Mary, all the saints, and all of our family and friends.

Scripture and tradition use all kinds of images to describe heaven:

- a heavenly city (Revelation 21:2)
- a glorious wedding celebration (Matthew 22:1–14)
- a beautiful paradise (Luke 23:43)

How have you heard heaven described?

Even these beautiful images only hint at the amazing beauty and remarkable happiness of heaven. The true beauty of heaven is "beyond all understanding" (*CCC* 1027).

What Is Hell?

Heaven is a place where we are totally surrounded by God's love. **Hell** is a place where God's love is absent. Those who say no to God's love and refuse his mercy end up in hell. God doesn't want anyone to go to hell. But God won't force us to love him if we don't want to. The worst thing about hell is that we're separated from God, who loves us forever.

We can join in the prayer of the Church that "no one should be lost" in hell (*CCC* 1058).

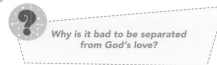

Why is it bad to be separated from God's love?

What Is Heaven?

Ask the children to answer the reflection question on their own using what they've just learned in this section about what the Church teaches heaven is.

Ask the students if their understanding of heaven changed from the beginning of class. If so, how? If not, what stayed the same and why?

What Is Hell?

Discuss the reflection question as a group. If the children need prompting to help answer the question, ask them what God's love gives us (*grace, courage, guidelines for living a life like Jesus, freedom from sin, eternal life, and so on*) and what life might be like without those things. Then ask the reflection question again.

What Is Purgatory?

Not everyone who dies loving God is ready to go to heaven. Some of us need more time to get ready. **Purgatory** is a place where we're purified, or prepared, for going to heaven. Time in purgatory makes us pure and holy so we can join God and the saints in heaven.

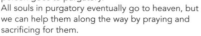

If we follow Jesus on earth, the Holy Spirit is purifying us from sin as we live. When someone dies before the Holy Spirit has finished, that person goes to purgatory. All souls in purgatory eventually go to heaven, but we can help them along the way by praying and sacrificing for them.

A PRAYER

Pray this prayer for someone you know and love who has died:

Eternal rest grant unto [name], O Lord.
And let perpetual light shine upon
    [him/her].
And may the souls of all the faithful
    departed,
through the mercy of God, rest in peace.
Amen.

What Happens When Jesus Comes Back?

This world isn't eternal like heaven. Eventually, the whole world will come to an end. When the world ends, Jesus will come again. The first time, Jesus came in humility as a baby. He lived a life of service and died for us on the cross. In his Second Coming, Jesus will come in great glory and power. He will be accompanied by angels and saints. Everyone will recognize Jesus as the Lord and king of the universe. We don't know when Jesus will return, but he promised us he would.

When Jesus comes again, our souls and our bodies will live forever with God. God will transform our physical bodies into beautiful new creations that will never get sick or die. Even the bodies of those who have already died will be resurrected as new.

After the resurrection of the dead comes the **Final Judgment**. Every person who has ever lived will be judged, and we will see the consequences for every good or bad action we've ever done. Jesus will judge every bad deed and reward every good deed.

ACTIVITY

Write down three kind deeds you can do for someone else this week.

1. _____

_____

_____

2. _____

_____

_____

3. _____

_____

_____

What Is Purgatory?

If the children have a hard time understanding the concept of purgatory, you can compare it to other things we have to prepare for here on earth. For example, children have to go through middle school before they can go to high school or they have to learn the basics of music before they can have a solo.

What Happens When Jesus Comes Back?

Give the children time to complete the reflection activity on their own or with a partner. Go around the room and ask each child (or pair) to share one of the kind deeds on their list.

Final Activity

Give the children time at the end of the lesson to work on the final activity. Let them know they can use the art supplies and extra paper you've provided. Encourage the students to include elements in their artwork that you talked about in class today. Heaven may have lots of flowers, like a wedding celebration Matthew 22:1–14; purgatory may have a clock, like a waiting room; and hell might be dark, away from God's light. Walk around the room as children work to see what they create. You could even hang some of this artwork up around the room or somewhere else on the parish campus to share with parishioners.

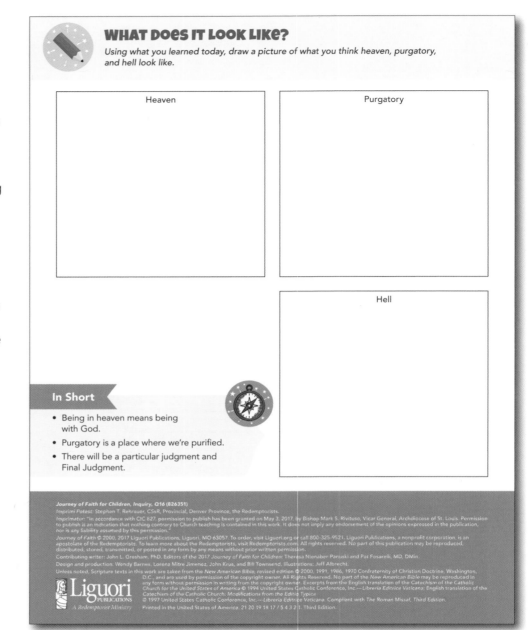

WHAT DOES IT LOOK LIKE?

Using what you learned today, draw a picture of what you think heaven, purgatory, and hell look like.

Heaven

Purgatory

Hell

In Short

- Being in heaven means being with God.
- Purgatory is a place where we're purified.
- There will be a particular judgment and Final Judgment.

Journey of Faith for Children, Inquiry, Q16 (826351)
Imprimi Potest: Stephen T. Rehrauer, CSsR, Provincial, Denver Province, the Redemptorists.
Imprimatur: "In accordance with CIC 827, permission to publish has been granted on May 3, 2017, by Bishop Mark S. Rivituso, Vicar General, Archdiocese of St. Louis. Permission to publish is an indication that nothing contrary to Church teaching is contained in this work. It does not imply any endorsement of the opinions expressed in the publication, nor is any liability assumed by this permission."
Journey of Faith © 2000, 2017 Liguori Publications, Liguori, MO 63057. To order, visit Liguori.org or call 800-325-9521. Liguori Publications, a nonprofit corporation, is an apostolate of the Redemptorists. To learn more about the Redemptorists, visit Redemptorists.com. All rights reserved. No part of this publication may be reproduced, distributed, stored, transmitted, or posted in any form by any means without prior written permission.
Contributing writer: John L. Gresham, PhD. Editors of the 2017 Journey of Faith for Children: Theresa Nienaber-Panuski and Pat Fosarelli, MD, DMin.
Design and production: Wendy Barnes, Lorena Mitre Jimenez, John Krus, and Bill Townsend. Illustrations: Jeff Albrecht.
Unless noted, Scripture texts in this work are taken from the *New American Bible*, revised edition © 2010, 1991, 1986, 1970 Confraternity of Christian Doctrine, Washington, D.C., and are used by permission of the copyright owner. All Rights Reserved. No part of the *New American Bible* may be reproduced in any form without permission in writing from the copyright owner. Excerpts from the English translation of the *Catechism of the Catholic Church* for the United States of America © 1994 United States Catholic Conference, Inc.—Libreria Editrice Vaticana; English translation of the *Catechism of the Catholic Church*: Modifications from the *Editio Typica* © 1997 United States Catholic Conference, Inc.—Libreria Editrice Vaticana. Compliant with *The Roman Missal, Third Edition*.
Printed in the United States of America. 21 20 19 18 17 / 5 4 3 2 1. Third Edition.

Liguori PUBLICATIONS
A Redemptorist Ministry

Closing Prayer

Lead the children in the prayer found on the lesson handout. If there is a deceased member of the parish to pray for, use his or her name. Otherwise, you can just use "them" for the blanks in the prayer.

Eternal rest grant unto [name],
*   O Lord.*
And let perpetual light
*   shine upon [him/her].*
And may the souls of all the
*   faithful departed,*
through the mercy of God,
*   rest in peace. Amen.*

Take-Home

Ask the children to lead the prayer in their lesson handout that you used for your closing prayer with their families before or after a family meal. They can pray it especially for someone they know who has died or for all the souls in purgatory.

Journey of Faith for Children
Inquiry Glossary (alphabetical)

Advent: The beginning of the liturgical year. It begins on the fourth Sunday before Christmas and ends before the first evening prayer of Christmas on Christmas Eve. This season emphasizes the coming (advent or arrival) of Jesus Christ, joy, hope, repentance, expectation, and preparation. The first part of Advent highlights his Second Coming at the end of time, and the second part (December 17–24) his coming into human history by his birth.

alb: A Latin word for "white," this long white garment is symbolic of the total purity that should cover one in one's approach to God. It is worn by the celebrant (priest), a deacon, and those who serve as lectors, servers, acolytes, or other lay ministers.

Alleluia: Meaning "praise the Lord" in Hebrew, this word is used frequently during the Easter season and is recited or sung before the reading of the Gospel (except during Lent) to emphasize the presence of Jesus in the word of God.

altar: The central table on which the Communion bread and the cup of wine are offered as the eucharistic sacrifice. The altar "represents the two aspects of the same mystery: the altar of the sacrifice and the table of the Lord" (*CCC* 1383).

altar server: Assists at the altar during liturgies by carrying the cross or processional candles, holding the book for the celebrant when needed, carrying the incense and censer, presenting the bread, wine, and water during the preparation of the gifts, washing the hands of the priest, and any other necessary tasks. Altar servers can be male or female but must have received their first Communion before participating as a server.

ambo: An elevated pulpit from which the Scriptures are proclaimed during Mass.

archbishop: A bishop who oversees an archdiocese.

archdiocese: A large diocese overseen by an archbishop.

associate pastor: Also known as parochial vicar, a priest who assists a pastor in the parish (see **pastor**).

auxiliary bishop: A helper bishop who assists in large dioceses (see **bishop**).

baptism: A sacrament of the Catholic Church that takes away original sin and makes an individual a member of Christ's body, the Church.

baptismal font: A large basin or small pool that contains the blessed water used for baptizing. Every parish church should have a baptismal font, which is usually set in a prominent and visible place in the church building.

Bible: Also called sacred Scripture or the Scriptures, it is a collection of books accepted by the Church as the inspired, authentic account of God's self-revelation and plan of salvation for the human race. It is divided into the Old Testament and New Testament (see **Old Testament** and **New Testament**).

bishop: The chief pastor and head of a specific diocese. According to the Second Vatican Council, the bishop is called to "eminently and visibly take the place of Christ himself, teacher, shepherd and priest, and act in his person" (Dogmatic Constitution on the Church [*Lumen Gentium*], 21).

brother (religious): A man who is a member of a religious order but is not ordained. The *Catechism* states that religious life is "one way of experiencing a 'more intimate' consecration, rooted in Baptism and dedicated totally to God" (*CCC* 916).

candidate: Someone already baptized in the Christian faith seeking to become a full member of the Catholic Church.

canonization: The final declaration by the pope that a person is a saint, in heaven, and worthy of veneration by all the faithful. This step is normally preceded by beatification and the authentication of two miracles ascribed to him or her by the Church.

cantor: A member of the church choir who leads the congregation in song.

cardinal: Canon law describes the cardinals as those who "constitute a special college which provides for the election of the Roman Pontiff....The cardinals assist the Roman Pontiff either collegially...or individually when they help the Roman Pontiff through the various offices they perform" (*Canon* 349). Cardinal is an honorary title, and cardinals are normally bishops.

Catechism of the Catholic Church: A summary or manual containing the basics of Christian doctrine. The *Catechism of the Catholic Church* was commissioned by a synod of bishops in 1986 and first published in English in 1994 for the purpose of "faithfully and systematically present[ing] the teaching of Sacred Scripture, the living Tradition of the Church and the authentic Magisterium" (*Fidei Depositum*).

catechist: Someone who instructs and forms others in the Catholic faith either in preparation for baptism or continuing instruction and formation for those who are already baptized.

catechumen: An unbaptized person seeking to become a full member of the Catholic Church.

catechumenate: The period of instruction and involvement in the Catholic faith in preparation for the baptism of adults or for the reception of baptized non-Catholics. Those preparing to receive baptism and admission into the Church are called catechumens.

chasuble: The outermost garment worn by the priest in the celebration of Mass.

Christmas: Also called the feast of the Nativity of Jesus Christ, celebrated on December 25. Many of the customs surrounding Christmas have origins in pagan celebrations but have been "christened" with religious significance.

Church year: Beginning with the first Sunday of Advent, followed by the Christmas season, Ordinary Time, Lent, the Easter Triduum, the Easter season, and ending with Ordinary Time, this calendar "unfolds the whole mystery of Christ" (Constitution on the Sacred Liturgy [*Sacrosanctum Concilium*], 102). (See **Advent, Christmas, Ordinary Time, Lent, Triduum, Easter.**)

Communion: Also called the holy Eucharist, this is a sacrament of the Catholic Church where believers receive the true presence of Jesus Christ in the form of bread and wine. This sacrament usually occurs within the context of the holy Mass.

communion of saints: All the members of Christ's body, the Church, in heaven, in purgatory, and on earth.

confessional: The place in a church set aside for celebration of the sacrament of penance. The penitent has the option of confessing to the priest face to face or anonymously behind a screen.

confirmation: A sacrament of initiation where a Catholic is anointed with holy oil and made a full, adult member of the Catholic Church. During this sacrament the Holy Spirit comes to dwell in the heart of the recipient in a special way and blesses the recipient with special graces.

convent: The building housing a community of religious sisters.

crucifix: A cross with the image of Jesus as suffering Savior. Catholics find the blessed crucifix a revered object of private or public devotion as a reminder of the triumphant suffering of Christ.

deacon: A member of the clergy who is ordained for service to the people of God, ranked under bishops and priests. The role of the deacon is to serve the corporal and spiritual needs of the community and to assist in preaching the word of God. There are two types of deacons: transitional and permanent.

diocese: "A community of the Christian faithful in communion of faith and sacraments with the bishop ordained in apostolic succession" (*CCC* 833). A diocese serves a specific geographical area and is led by a bishop. Parishes make up a diocese and are led by pastors.

divine revelation: God's self-revelation to humankind. Both sacred Scripture and tradition are part of divine revelation.

Easter: A movable feast celebrated on a Sunday between March 22 and April 25. This feast celebrates the resurrection of Jesus Christ from the dead. It is considered the greatest of all Christian feasts; the Easter season continues for fifty days from Easter Sunday to the feast of Pentecost (see *CCC* 1170).

Easter candle: A large candle symbolic of the risen Savior, the Light of the World. It is blessed on Holy Saturday and remains lit throughout the Easter season during liturgical services.

epistles: Also called letters, they make up a large part of the New Testament. The epistles are commonly divided into the Pauline letters and the Catholic letters. The Pauline letters were written by St. Paul or by his disciples in his name. The Catholic letters were written to a more universal audience by various authors from the year 65 to about 95.

eucharistic minister: Gives Communion at Mass and is trained to take Communion to people who are sick or homebound.

eucharistic prayer: The prayer of the priest when he asks God to accept and bless the gifts of bread and wine during Mass.

extraordinary minister of holy Communion: Someone who is named to administer the Eucharist after it has been consecrated ("made sacred") by a priest or the person celebrating the Mass.

faith: Both a grace and the human act of knowing and living like we are loved and cherished by God. The *Catechism* expands on this by saying that "'Faith *seeks understanding*'; it is intrinsic to faith that a believer desires to know better the One in whom he has put his faith….The grace of faith opens 'the eyes of your hearts' to a lively understanding of the contents of Revelation" (*CCC* 158).

Father (God the): The first person of the Holy Trinity. God the Father was revealed first to the people of Israel in the Old Testament.

feast days: Days designated for remembrance and celebration of a saint, holy person, or event that has special significance to the Church.

Final Judgment: As spoken of in the New Testament, the Final or General Judgment is the final encounter with Christ at his Second Coming, during which all of humanity will be judged.

genuflect: The action of briefly kneeling with one knee on the floor and blessing yourself with the Sign of the Cross while facing the tabernacle.

Gloria: An ancient hymn of praise that begins with the song of the angels from St. Luke's account of the birth of Christ.

godparent: Someone who is chosen by the candidate being baptized or parents of the child being baptized to serve as a mentor in the faith. A godparent must be at least sixteen years old, an actively practicing Catholic, and willing to take on the commitment of walking alongside the newly baptized on the road of Christian life.

Gospel: Meaning "good news," a Gospel is one of the four divinely inspired accounts of the life, teaching, suffering, death, and resurrection of Jesus Christ. The Gospels comprise the books of Matthew, Mark, Luke, and John.

hallowed: To recognize and treat something as holy, or to give honor or reverence to.

heaven: Eternal life with God and the saints. Heaven is the ultimate goal of human life.

hell: A state of "definitive self-exclusion from communion with God and the blessed" (*CCC* 1033). To be in hell after death requires someone to die in mortal sin freely choosing to refuse to repent and rejecting God's merciful love.

Holy, Holy, Holy: A song of praise to God taken from the Book of Isaiah that begins the eucharistic prayer.

holy days of obligation: Days set aside for the worship of God. This includes each Sunday of the year and other feast days designated by the Church. All Catholics are required to participate in the Mass on these days.

Holy Spirit (God the): The third person of the Holy Trinity. God the Holy Spirit is the advocate Jesus promised before his ascension into heaven. The Holy Spirit descended upon the apostles during Pentecost.

holy water: Water that is blessed by a priest for use by Catholics. It is used most often to make the Sign of the Cross while blessing oneself. Holy water is a reminder of baptism and symbolic of spiritual cleansing.

homily: Usually, but not always, given by the presider of the Mass, it is an instruction or sermon designed to explain the day's Scripture readings and how to apply them meaningfully today.

initiation: To start something, or something you have to go through before becoming an official part of or full member of a group or organization.

inspired (or **divine inspiration**): The books of the Bible are considered divinely inspired because their authors were inspired to write through the grace and help of the Holy Spirit.

inquiry: The first stage of the RCIA. In this stage, the inquirer is learning about Christ, the Church, prayer, the saints, and the Christian way of life. The purpose of this stage is for the inquirer to grow and develop in faith and to determine if he or she desires to move forward in the RCIA process.

laity: Those members of the Church who are not ordained in holy orders. The laity are called to witness the faith with their lives.

lectern: A wood or metal podium from which all nonscriptural readings and singing are led.

Lectionary: A book containing a three-year cycle of Scripture readings for Sundays and some feasts, a two-year weekday cycle, a one-year cycle for saints feast days, and readings for ritual Masses and Masses for particular intentions.

lector: Someone who proclaims the Scripture readings, except for the Gospels, in liturgical worship.

Lent: The penitential season beginning on Ash Wednesday and ending before the Mass on Holy Thursday.

Liturgy of the Eucharist: The second main part of the eucharistic celebration of the Latin rite. It begins with the presentation of the bread and wine and prayers of offering by the priest. Next the priest recites a prayer of thanksgiving, the congregation responds with the "Holy, Holy, Holy," and the eucharistic prayer. This is followed by the Communion rite, final prayers, and the sending forth of the people.

Liturgy of the Word: The first main part of the eucharistic celebration of the Latin rite. It includes the proclamation of the word of God, a homily on the Scriptures, the recitation of the Creed, and the offering of petitions.

miracle: A sign or wonder, such as healing or the control of nature, which can only be attributed to divine power. The miracles of Jesus were messianic signs of the presence of God's kingdom.

monastery: A place where religious live in seclusion from the outside world. It can be applied to religious communities of both men and women but is commonly used to describe the home of monks or other religious men who live a cloistered life.

monk: A male religious who is a member of a monastic community. Common monastic orders in the Church include the Benedictines, the Cistercians, and the Carthusians.

music minister: One who helps to lead music during the liturgy.

mystagogy: This is the final stage of the RCIA, which continues until Pentecost and is a period of postbaptismal catechesis. The purpose of mystagogy is to allow the newly baptized to reflect on their baptism, learn more about their new faith, and explore the ways they may be called to serve the Church in the world and their parish.

New Testament: Contains twenty-seven books written in Greek between the years 50 and 140. It includes the four Gospels, the Acts of the Apostles, the epistles of St. Paul, other epistles, and the Book of Revelation. The major theme of the New Testament is Jesus Christ: his person, preaching, saving death and resurrection, and relationship to us.

nun: While commonly used to describe any female religious, this term actually applies only to those who live the monastic life or in a cloister that restricts contact with the outside world.

offertory: When the unconsecrated bread and wine are brought to the altar and prepared as an offering to God.

Old Testament: Contains forty-six books, written in Hebrew between the years 900 BC and 160 BC. Included are books with distinct purposes: historical, moral, and prophetic. These books are a record of God's relationship with the Israelites, "the Chosen People," and of their responses to the divine plan.

Ordinary Time: The period in the liturgical year between the end of the Christmas season and the beginning of Lent, and the Monday after Pentecost until the beginning of Advent.

parish: A geographical area within a diocese that has been assigned its own church and pastor.

parish center: The building on a parish campus where the day-to-day business of the parish is taken care of.

particular judgment: The moment after death when God reviews our lives and we are sent to either heaven, purgatory, or hell.

pastor: According to canon law, "The pastor is the proper (shepherd) of the parish entrusted to him, exercising the pastoral care of the community committed to him under the authority of the diocesan bishop in whose ministry of Christ he has been called to share...he carries out the functions of teaching, sanctifying, and governing, also with the cooperation of other presbyters or deacons and with the assistance of lay members of the Christian faithful" (*Canon* 519). (See also **associate pastor**.)

patron saints: Saints who are considered patrons of specific groups or causes.

Pentecost: The last day of the Easter season during the Church year. On this day we remember how the Holy Spirit came to the apostles and made them strong, wise, and eager to build the Church.

Pentateuch: Also known as the Torah, this is the name given to the first five books of the Bible: Genesis, Exodus, Leviticus, Numbers, and Deuteronomy.

person: When used in reference to the Holy Trinity, person refers to one of the three persons of God: Father, Son, or Holy Spirit.

petitions: (See **Universal Prayer**.)

pew: The long bench you sit in during Mass. All pews in the church should face the altar.

pope: This is the title of the bishop of Rome, the successor of St. Peter, the apostle Jesus named as the head of the apostles and the head of the Church. As the head of the Church, the pope leads as the shepherd of all the faithful in his care.

priest: A man who is ordained through the sacrament of holy orders to serve the faithful. He has the authority to perform the sacraments and celebrate the Mass.

procession: A group of people moving together as part of a celebration or special event. During Mass, there is an entrance processional and a closing processional.

purgatory: The transitional state where souls judged worthy of heaven but imperfect at the time of death will undergo a final purification.

purification and enlightenment: This is the third period of the RCIA and the final period leading up to the Easter Vigil and reception of the sacraments. This period emphasizes prayer by both those seeking initiation into the Church and the parish community, as well as a further opportunity for study and spiritual direction.

reconciliation room: (See **confessional**.)

rectory: The residence of the priests serving a parish.

religious order: Organized groups of religious who live and work together under a unique charism and with specific ministries in which members take part (prayer, service, teaching, health care, and so on). Those in a religious order generally take vows of poverty, chastity, and obedience.

Responsorial Psalm: A psalm, which almost always comes from the Book of Psalms, sung or recited during Mass between the first and second readings on Sundays and major feast days, or between the first reading and the Gospel on other days.

Rite of Christian Initiation of Adults: The Rite of Christian Initiation of Adults (RCIA) is the process of becoming a member of the Catholic Church for those beyond the age of reason. The rite begins with a participant's entry into the catechumenate and culminates in the celebration of the sacraments of initiation.

rite: A serious, religious ceremony based in tradition.

Roman Missal, The: Also called the *Sacramentary*, this is a book of prayers and directives for the celebration of the Mass and other sacraments.

rosary: A meditation on the events (called "Mysteries") in the life of Jesus and Mary includes the Joyful, Sorrowful, Glorious, and Luminous.

sacraments: Rituals in the Catholic Church that have grown from Christ's teaching during his time on earth. A sacrament is a physical sign of God's intangible presence with his Church on earth.

sacraments of initiation: The sacraments received to become a full member of the Catholic Church: baptism, confirmation, and the Eucharist.

sacristy: A room near or in the church used to store sacred vessels and other materials used in the liturgy. This room is also used by the priest and other church ministers to prepare for Mass and other services.

saint: A person who has lived a holy life, is in heaven, and is honored by the universal Church (see **canonization**).

sanctuary lamp: A light or candle kept burning at all times whenever the Blessed Sacrament is present. This light can usually be found near the tabernacle.

seminary: A school for men who want to train to become priests.

sister (religious): A woman who is a member of a religious order. The *Catechism* states that religious life is "one way of experiencing a 'more intimate' consecration, rooted in baptism and dedicated totally to God" (*CCC* 916).

Son (God the): The second person of the Trinity. God the Son came to earth in the person of Jesus Christ to save God's people from sin. The teachings of Jesus can be found in the New Testament.

sponsor: It is the sponsor's role to offer support and encouragement during the RCIA process and then to present the candidate when it is time for the candidate to receive the sacraments. The requirements for a sponsor are the same as for a godparent.

stole: A thin band of material worn around the neck and shoulders, symbolic of the "yoke of the Lord." Priests wear a stole during the celebration of all the sacraments. Deacons may wear a stole only diagonally over the shoulder.

tabernacle: A special place where the consecrated Eucharist is kept. The tabernacle should be located in a visible and prominent place in the church.

Torah: Also known as the Pentateuch, this is the name given to the first five books of the Bible: Genesis, Exodus, Leviticus, Numbers, and Deuteronomy.

trespasses: To commit an act, or sin, against God or another person.

Triduum: The Easter Triduum is the central celebration of the Church year and includes the three celebrations leading up to Easter, namely the Mass of the Lord's Supper on Holy Thursday, the celebration of the Passion of the Lord on Good Friday, and the Easter Vigil on Holy Saturday night.

Trinity, Holy: The doctrine that states there are three persons in one God, the Father, Son, and Holy Spirit, and that they are eternally united in a communion of love.

Universal Prayer: The offering of prayers to God by the faithful during Mass. These prayers usually include petitions for the holy Church, those who govern the Church, those suffering for various needs, the community, and the world.

usher: Someone who greets people before and after Mass, helps them find a seat, and collects the offertory gifts. Ushers may also assist with the Communion lines.

vestments: Symbolic garments worn by priests and deacons during liturgical celebrations.

womb: The biological part of a woman where a child grows before birth.

yoke: A wooden crosspiece that is fastened over the necks of two animals and attached to the plow or cart that they are to pull. "Yoke of the Lord" signifies that the one who wears it is doing hard work for God.